What people are saying about …

# THE DATING MANIFESTO

"Lisa Anderson is one of those delightfully blunt people who makes you laugh and think. She's funny and smart. But better than that: She has wisdom to offer. And—especially when it comes to relationship issues—that's in short supply. It's worth buying this book for chapter 11 alone. People need to hear this."

**Brant Hansen,** radio host, author of *Unoffendable*, and storyteller for CURE International

"A wise book from a woman who understands the pressures of Christian dating and singleness as well as anyone in the world. Lisa's fun personality, concern for others, depth of thought, and no-nonsense approach to life and love are on fu'' ... ... I loved *The Dating Manifesto* and am giving a copy ... ... ...ters."

... ... f *Sacred*

... *Search*

"Reading *The Dating Manif...* ... ...wn for a cup of coffee with an older, wiser, funnier ... ...sa challenges singles to stop making excuses and start taking responsibility for their lives and relationships. If you're single, this is a book that will both challenge you and encourage you."

**Debra Fileta, MA, LPC,** author of
*True Love Dates*, TrueLoveDates.com

"Lisa is saying what few others—married or single—in the church are willing to say. I appreciate the wit, wisdom, and candor that she brings to Focus on the Family's Boundless ministry on a daily basis. *The Dating Manifesto* is essential reading for single men and women, as well as for anyone who cares about them."

**Jim Daly,** president of Focus on the Family

"If I ever start dating again, I'm going to use this advice."

**Dorothy Anderson,** Lisa's 86-year-old mom

"In today's culture, there's no question that dating is a potential minefield—and that's why Lisa's advice is so invaluable. With her trademark humor and refreshing honesty, Lisa offers singles a road map for pursuing healthy relationships in a God-honoring way. Singles and married people alike will benefit from her solid biblical perspective."

**Greg Smalley,** vice president of family
ministries at Focus on the Family

"Wow! Lisa Anderson has written a book I will stock and hand out to singles every chance I get. Her witty writing style makes this treatise on marriage feel like entertainment, but she hits the bull's-eye with meaty, truth-filled content and practical advice. I love that

Lisa has kept her heart open to marriage but has not made it the end-all goal of her life."

**Dannah Gresh,** bestselling author
of *And the Bride Wore White*

"*The Dating Manifesto* is the quintessential dating manual that single Christians need to keep at the ready. It's relevant, straightforward, and engaging from cover to cover. Some parts were so painfully real that they broke my heart; other parts were so hilarious that I embarrassed myself by laughing out loud in public. Lisa doesn't shy away from the beauty of biblical truth or the way it collides with the hard realities of life as a single person. I intend to buy several copies and give them out to single friends."

**Joshua Rogers,** writer and attorney, blogger
at JoshuaRogers.com and Boundless.org

# THE DATING MANIFESTO

# THE DATING MANIFESTO

## A DRAMA-FREE PLAN FOR PURSUING MARRIAGE WITH PURPOSE

lisa ANDERSON

★ ★ ★ ★ ★ ★ ★

David C Cook

*transforming lives together*

THE DATING MANIFESTO
Published by David C Cook
4050 Lee Vance View
Colorado Springs, CO 80918 U.S.A.

David C Cook Distribution Canada
55 Woodslee Avenue, Paris, Ontario, Canada N3L 3E5

David C Cook U.K., Kingsway Communications
Eastbourne, East Sussex BN23 6NT, England

The graphic circle C logo is a registered trademark of David C Cook.

The website addresses recommended throughout this book are offered as a
resource to you. These websites are not intended in any way to be or imply an
endorsement on the part of David C Cook, nor do we vouch for their content.

All Scripture quotations are taken from The Holy Bible, English Standard
Version® (ESV®), copyright © 2001 by Crossway, a publishing ministry
of Good News Publishers. Used by permission. All rights reserved.

LCCN 2014959544
ISBN 978-1-4347-0887-8
eISBN 978-1-4347-0935-6

The Team: Ingrid Beck, Nicci Hubert, Nick Lee, Tiffany Thomas, Karen Athen
Cover Design: Amy Konyndyk and Nick Lee

Printed in the United States of America
First Edition 2015

1 2 3 4 5 6 7 8 9 10

052915

*To Julianna and Amie*
*Thanks for living this story alongside me.*

# CONTENTS

# ACKNOWLEDGMENTS

I've described this book to friends as "the book I never intended to write but finally had to." I'm pretty sure I've spoken this book in some form about a thousand times, if not more. These thoughts have surfaced over the past months and years at meals, in meetings, at parties, in relationship interventions, during breakup sob fests, on group hikes, at church potlucks, in small group discussions, at speaking engagements, and beyond.

This book finally became the monkey on my back that I had to either shake off or put in print. And so here we are. But I wouldn't be here without the input, prayer, and support of many. Too many to list here, but I'll recognize a few.

First, thanks be to God. I've been asked what it's like to be a "strong, confident woman." Honestly, there are only two real reasons I'm confident: my salvation is secure, and I'm unconditionally loved by my Creator. Everything else is just personality and lesser things. Because of Christ, I have a future, a hope, and a purpose for the present. I can walk the road I'm on with full assurance that my steps are guided by a God who is all-powerful and all good. Who could ask for anything more? Thanks, Lord, for being the God who sees a single girl who at times feels unseen. I want my life and this book to be for your glory alone.

Mom, you're simply the best. You've walked through life with me as a mother, friend, confidant, and prayer warrior. Thanks for believing in me, rooting for me, and hoping with me for marriage and more. And yes, I know I'm still The Fav.

Dad, you did the same. Since you're with Jesus now and haven't seen where I've come since I was younger, dumber, and floundering a good bit, I'll fill you in when I get to heaven.

Laura, Tina, Sara, Martha, and Phil, thanks for being my family and for inviting me into your families. I couldn't ask for better siblings, and I am who I am, in large part, because of you.

Julianna, Amie, Christina, Wendy, Heather, Sara, Jeni, Jenn, Julie, the Bible study girls, and every other woman who has walked, prayed, cried, yelled, and laughed through my journey with me, you own a piece of this book. Thanks for being my tribe.

Martha and Anthony, thanks for living and breathing these principles with me at Boundless.org. I'm excited by what God is doing in and through you, and you both make coming to work each day a joy. Dave, your rockin' audio skills make up for your snarky humor. Greg, thanks for being a life-giving boss who joined the chorus in telling me to write this book. My Focus on the Family family, I can't think of better people to surround myself with each day.

Steve, Candice, Motte, and Ted, thanks for introducing me to Boundless and to a whole new way of looking at dating and marriage. You helped revolutionize my thinking on this subject.

Alex, Paul, and Glenn, thanks for being my book buddies and sharing your expertise on the biz. You are pros, and your tips gave me much-needed know-how to move forward.

Ginia, you championed this book before it was written. Thanks for making it finally happen. The team at David C Cook: Ingrid, Amy, Nick, Nicci, Leigh, Tim, Darren, Karla, Tiffany, Michelle, Channing, Lisa, Blythe, Karen, and Dennis—you make producing a book look easy. Thanks for your talent and encouragement along the way.

To the friends and fans of Boundless and *The Boundless Show* worldwide, you were instrumental in my reaching the finish line. Your stories inspire me; your determination to mature and marry well brings me joy. Thanks especially to those who've said you pray for me daily—for wisdom, courage, and even my future marriage. I love you all.

Finally, to the reader of this book, thanks for hearing me out in these pages. Thanks for taking in my story and my lessons learned. I still find it hard to believe that this book is in your hands. But I'm grateful. May God use it, even in a small way, to accomplish something great in your life.

# PROLOGUE
## NO SINGLE RIDERS

It was a dark and stormy night.

Okay, not really. It was dark, but pretty warm and quiet on that mid-September evening. I had attended a meeting after work, then met a friend for a late dinner. Now driving home with my moonroof open and stereo blaring, I looked forward to nothing more than walking through my front door, showering, and tumbling into bed.

That's when I saw it.

It danced at the corner of my eye at first. It was unusual—out of place. I felt immediately that something was different, that this well-worn route in the middle of town had a new attraction. Only when I approached the busy intersection and glanced left did I behold it in all its glory.

A carnival.

Yes, the picture you have in your head right now is spot on. This was *that* kind of carnival. The kind that blows into town from some nondescript city, attracts seedy characters, violates health and safety codes, employs ex-cons, and lures unsuspecting single women on their way home from late meetings and dinners with friends.

Perhaps it was the bright lights, or more likely the fact that I love anything that smacks of an amusement park (because as a member of generation X, amusing myself rates pretty high on my list of priorities), but I decided immediately that I was going to ride the Ferris wheel. I'm not sure why I chose the Ferris wheel; probably because the vision of my cackling gleefully by myself on the Scrambler was embarrassing. Or worse, my riding the Himalaya, the deafening squeal of '70s arena rock music shaking the entire structure, and answering the ride operator's shout of "Do you wanna go *faaaaaaaster*?" with *"Yeeeeaaaaaaaah!"*

But here I was at my spontaneous best: the Lisa who leaves margin for fun, creates experiences, and laughs in the face of self-consciousness and convention; the Lisa I wish I were far more often. Fun Lisa quickly cut across two lanes of traffic to swing into the carnival's parking lot. I parked, stepped out of my car, slammed the door shut, and threw my keys into my purse. Blissfully unconcerned that I was still in a pencil skirt and heels after a long day at the office, I strode purposefully toward the carnival entrance.

I looked at my watch; it was almost ten o'clock. I probably should've questioned the wisdom of a girl wandering alone through a carnival late at night, but it honestly never crossed my mind. The scene before me was pretty empty, and most of the rides were eerily motionless, including the Ferris wheel. Still, as I stepped up to a rickety booth to purchase my tokens, the attendant assured me that the Ferris wheel was good to go; it just needed riders.

The wheel loomed above me as I approached it. Its red and yellow lights danced (the ones that weren't burned out; this wasn't Disneyland, people), synchronized to a gurgling tune that made me think of acrobats and cotton candy. The ride operator was slumped against the gate, smoking. My mind flew back many years to the time I asked a carnival ride operator how he determined the length of a ride. "You're done when I've smoked two cigarettes," he replied smoothly. I was hoping for at least a two-cigarette ride tonight.

"Hi!" I called out eagerly, fixing a grin on Smokey. "Hey," he said. I ignored his unwillingness to match my enthusiasm; I was too busy picturing myself moments from now, floating above the city while reflecting on my day and maybe talking to God a bit. Maybe I'd rattle off what I was thankful for. Maybe I'd make a mental list of goals to accomplish in the coming weeks. Perhaps I'd even allow myself a moment of self-congratulation, a certain smugness for being so carpe diem. *I make things happen. It is so cool to be me.*

"I wanna ride the Ferris wheel!" I said as I held out my hand, exposing the five tokens representing the ridiculous sum I'd agreed to pay for one ride.

"Cool," said Smokey. "But you need someone else to ride with you."

"Oh," I said. *I guess that makes sense,* I thought. After all, I was the only one there, and if I were the owner of a seedy carnival, I'd do my best to turn a profit. Operating a Ferris wheel for just one person obviously wouldn't accomplish that. How much does it cost to operate a Ferris wheel, anyway? I'll have to google that. In the meantime, I waited.

I looked about for potential Ferris wheel comrades, but no one was nearby. I turned imploringly upon Smokey, and he just shrugged sadly. Lame. Of course this would happen to me. I drummed my fingers impatiently against the railing. Then, out of nowhere, a group of teens approached the ride.

"There!" I said triumphantly. "Now there are enough people, right?" I held my token-laden hand out once more.

"No, you need at least two people per *bucket*," he answered.

"You're joking, right?"

"I'm not. I'm sorry, lady. No single riders."

*Excuse me?* It was as if he'd announced at the top of his lungs that I had leprosy. Or a criminal record. Or an unhealthy obsession with Justin Bieber. I immediately felt self-conscious and—what's the word?—*ashamed*.

No single riders.

The teenagers, all of whom had witnessed the scene, whisked past me to get on the ride. One guy—he looked to be about sixteen, with meticulously gelled hair, pierced ears, and several nondescript tattoos—jerked a thumb at whom I assumed was his girlfriend as he turned to me and said, "If I wasn't with her, I would ride with you."

"Thanks," I mumbled, and turned away. He probably thought I was a mom whose kids had ditched her to hang out by the restrooms and text their friends. I scanned the area, looking down the corridor toward the rows of games and snack vendors. My hope was to find someone wandering about alone, someone whose companionship I could buy so I could have my wish.

I saw no one. Where was everybody? I glanced back at the Ferris wheel and saw Smokey, slumped against the gate, eyes half shut, still smoking. I'm pretty sure he'd already forgotten about me. I could hear the happy murmur of teen voices high above me in the night sky.

Deflated and feeling utterly foolish, I tossed the tokens into my purse, walked back to my car, and climbed inside. With my hands on the steering wheel, I burst into tears.

I had never felt more *single* in my entire life.

You see, I'm single. I always have been. And most of the time, I'm okay with it. But sometimes a night like that carnival night comes along.

That poor ride operator didn't know my heart. He didn't know my story. Neither did those carefree teenagers. It's not as if the carnival world conspired to make me feel terrible that evening. But as I drove home, endangering myself and other motorists with my tear-blurred vision, none of that mattered. What mattered was that I felt incredibly alone. And marginalized. And forgotten. Seen through the lens of my own story, the definition of *single rider* went in mere moments from "person riding the Ferris wheel solo" to "freakish single woman spurned by society, left to rot in her spinsterhood, isolated and unwanted."

I pulled into my garage, went into the house, powered up my computer, and sat down to record what happened; I didn't want to forget the details. I knew right then that if I ever wove my story into a book, the Ferris wheel debacle would be included.

Well, this is that book.

If you're single, you may feel as I did when I drove home from the carnival—that feeling of being forgotten, of being left behind, is palpable. Your life, and particularly your opposite-sex relationships, haven't turned out as you'd hoped. You wonder how you arrived where you are now, because it's not what you had planned in your head way back when you started dreaming. You're frustrated, maybe for good reason.

Or you may be in an entirely different place. You may be feeling pretty good about life right now. You're getting your feet wet, exploring all kinds of possibilities, dating a bit, or waiting to date until after you've lived life a little. Still, you're wondering if you really know all there is to know. You fear that you may be coasting, or even wasting time, and you don't know what to do about it.

If anything here sounds familiar, I'm talking to you. This book is not being written for my sake (though trust me, it'll be cathartic), but for yours. As the leader of a ministry for twenty- and thirtysomethings and the host of a show for singles, I often wish I had time to sit down with every person I've heard from, every guy or girl who's emailed me or found me on Facebook or chased me down at a conference and said, "Okay, Lisa, but what about …?"

This is that conversation. This is what I'd tell you if I had the luxury of talking with you nonstop for a week about singleness, dating, and preparing for marriage (as I've done with many of my long-suffering friends, bless their hearts). Because here's the truth: I'd like to be married.

How did I come to this realization in my own life? Good question. I was not the best marriage advocate in my twenties. I was probably the person I'm talking to now—the person I hope is reading this book.

When I was twenty-eight, I started work as a publicist for Focus on the Family. One of my internal clients was Boundless, Focus's ministry to single young adults. Boundless was founded in 1998 as a Webzine to guide college students in understanding and applying a biblical worldview to their lives. But over the years the audience aged into their twenties and thirties, and their interests ran more to navigating the world of dating and relationships.

Several years into my job, I became friends with the team that ran Boundless, a team made up primarily of three married guys with kids. I noticed right away that they were extremely passionate about the world of dating, and my first thought was, *Why?* I mean, they had each found someone, so wasn't it time to move on? Why did they care what a bunch of singles were up to? No other married folks I knew seemed to care about the world of the singleton. And what was the big deal about dating anyway? Most single people dated. Well, except for me.

It wasn't long before I found myself in long conversations with these guys. I started reading the articles on the Boundless website. I followed their blog. I listened and then voiced some opinions. Then I started voicing frustrations. I began sharing what I learned with my single girlfriends, and we'd discuss how it applied to our current situations. Why were we still single? Why weren't we dating? Why didn't we know many eligible Christian guys? Why did we rarely talk about marriage, hang out with married people, or treat marriage as something that was normative and (gulp) perhaps even a good thing?

All of these questions annoyed me, and I was at a loss on how to answer them. Where had I been the last fifteen years? What had I been doing? I was now in my midthirties and had been promoted a few times at work, taken on leadership positions at church, and even bought my first home. I was doing well. I was successful!

But now the Boundless team was in my face about marriage, and it made me feel weird because I didn't have any pat answers. I think one of them asked me if I had the gift of singleness. I didn't know—did I? I hoped not. But it's not as if I'd done any small groups or Bible studies on the subject. I probably assumed the gift of singleness was just for missionaries or people with difficult personalities; I certainly had never considered it for myself.

It turns out that one of the Boundless guys, Steve, had actually founded Boundless with his wife, Candice. Candice was now at home with their kids but still wrote for the site. Steve and Candice couldn't stop talking about marriage and family and shared their own dating and marriage story with me. They asked questions and challenged my assumptions. When I started dating a guy or two, Steve and Candice invited me over to talk about it. They got involved.

Before I knew it, I was talking about marriage a lot too. I began sitting down with my girlfriends to analyze their dating lives and awkwardly introduced the topic of marriage into conversations within my singles group. I read books about relationships and studied the Bible with new eyes.

I took a long, hard look at myself and my attitudes toward marriage—and men, for that matter. I had a lot to learn, and much to change. In fact, I still continue changing my behaviors and perceptions.

The thing that changed first was my willingness to acknowledge that marriage was a noble pursuit—one worth talking about. For the first time ever, I admitted my desire to be married. I spoke it out loud. I told my friends, including Steve and Candice. In January 2008, Boundless started a weekly podcast and asked me to host it. Since then, I've been admitting my desire for marriage to hundreds of thousands of single young adults each month.

There, I said it. I never wanted to be single for this long. I've never felt called to singleness. So what happened? I'm not totally sure. I know not all of it is within my control. But here's what I do know: I've learned things in recent years that I should've learned decades ago. I wish someone had taken me aside in my twenties and spelled out a few things. I wish they'd pulled no punches and had the courage to share their own mistakes. I wish people hadn't patted me on the head and left me alone to wander in the black hole of relationships. I wish, instead, they'd thrown up a few warning flags (or dismantled my vehicle altogether) as I veered off course.

I'm going to do that for you. I will say things I've heard very few others say, at least in the way I'll say them. I will tell it to you straight. I may offend you and will certainly surprise you.

In light of this, let me tell you what this book is not. This is not just another dating book. It's not a "follow your heart" book or fluffy, feel-good book. It's not a twelve-step program. It's not a "do these ten things and he or she will fall in love with you" book. It's not a whipping post for men, telling you you're hopeless—or worse, unnecessary. It's not a rallying cry for women, calling you to pick up your Hello Kitty coffee mugs for a toast to singleness and, in the meantime, to hold out for Mr. Right because he's "out there."

Here's what this book is: It's a vision of marriage from a person who isn't there yet. It's an argument for making marriage a priority even if right now it's the furthest thing from your mind. It's a brutal dismantling of our culture's (and in some ways, the church's) current dating system. It's advice for breaking the cycle you're in and starting fresh. It's also a challenge to thrive in your season of singleness, regardless of where you'll be down the road.

Perhaps most of all, this book is my arm around your shoulder. At forty-three and single, I'm right here with you. I don't have a so-called fairy-tale ending. Quite frankly, I don't know how my story will end; I only know I'm in the race with you—a few paces ahead, perhaps, but still running.

And this isn't a sprint, folks, it's a thoughtful and deliberate journey toward healthy change.

We have a lot of ground to cover, so let's get started.

# CHAPTER 1

# WHERE DID I GO WRONG?

My thirtieth birthday was a major bummer.

Major.

It's not just that I was turning thirty. In fact, most of my decade birthdays haven't bugged me too much. The fives (twenty-five and thirty-five) were harder for me. There's something about being on the downward slope toward the next decade that, in my opinion, is worse than actually getting there.

But thirty was a drag for a number of reasons. First, my dad had cancer. He'd been diagnosed about five months prior and had just finished his last round of chemo. He looked old and sick, and it was hard for me to look at him without breaking down. His skin was waxy, his voice weak and scratchy, and his bald head a signal to the world that all was not well. Seeing my dad so sick infused a lot of grief into a day that should have been hopeful and fun.

Second, I spent my thirtieth birthday at my uncle's funeral. Seven days earlier he'd been walking with my aunt through the airport, ready to board a flight to attend his grandson's high school graduation. Within seconds, he was on the floor of Concourse F, dead from a massive heart attack. Our family piled into cars and caravanned more than an hour's drive to a crowded country church to celebrate his life, grieve his departure, and comfort his wife and children.

At this point, my birthday was no longer about me, and rightly so. But I think my family felt sorry for me, because after the funeral we went back to my sister's place and had an impromptu barbecue. I was given cards and gifts, and everyone wished me well. My dad went upstairs for a nap. It was all pretty low key, which I guess is to be expected when you're turning thirty and sharing the day with a funeral.

As if this weren't enough to establish the day as one of the Top Ten Most Dismal Birthdays of All Time, something else sticks out about it.

It's the day I realized I was single.

Okay, I knew I was single before that day, of course. But I'd never really *noticed*. And I certainly hadn't cared—not really, anyway. But that day was different. It was the day life caught up with me, unceremoniously tapped me on the shoulder, and grabbed my attention.

I remember it so clearly: sitting on the sofa at my parents' house with a cup of coffee, silently wishing myself a happy birthday.

And then it popped into my head.

*I'm thirty and single. This isn't where I thought I'd be. This isn't the story I wanted or expected. What happened?*

I wasn't dating anyone. I wasn't even close to dating anyone. I had a good job, but I wasn't curing cancer, starting orphanages, or sharing the Gospel with unreached people groups. My job wasn't something that defined me, and I certainly wasn't too attached to it. My life was good, but it wasn't great. More accurately, it wasn't what I'd scripted for myself back when I thought life could be scripted. On that day I realized that during the past ten years, I'd abandoned the script and let myself drift. I'd dropped the reins and entered a desert, personally, professionally, and to some extent, spiritually.

So there I was at thirty, having a pre-midlife crisis. I thought by that age I'd be married. I thought I'd be fulfilling some kind of rockin' calling with a hopelessly devoted, incredibly hot, and financially secure husband who also happened to be ridiculously godly. Instead, I was an aging singleton with a sick dad, a dead uncle, and some serious questions about how I'd gotten there.

Where had I gone wrong?

## I'D LIKE TO BLAME MY CHILDHOOD

I always assumed I'd get married. Even in sixth grade I had relationship potential. It was the 1980s, and Tony, the school's best break-dancer, liked me. He was a big Filipino guy who held court outside in our school's commons, ghetto blaster by his side and broken-down refrigerator box at his feet to serve as his dance floor. He break-danced during recess as just about every kid in the school watched in awe. He was revered, at least as far as middle-school break-dancers go.

One day after an especially impressive show, he sauntered up to me in his parachute pants and Members Only jacket, nervously pulled a huge plastic comb from his pocket, swiped it through his gelled hair, and quietly asked me, right then and there, to be his girlfriend.

I smiled and said, "No."

It's not that I was trying to be mean. Even though I was pretty popular at school, I was generally kind. My rejecting Tony wasn't as much about him in *particular* as it was about him in *general*. You see, I was an honors student. I played first-chair flute in the band. I soloed in the choir. I had almost won the area spelling bee. (Should a sixth grader really be expected to spell *lieutenant*? Apparently so.) Basically what I'm saying is, I had *standards*. I was aiming higher than being the girlfriend of a break-dancer.

Then came Chad. Chad was everything Tony wasn't. Chad was a preppy kid from a rich family who was, in essence, John F. Kennedy Jr. His skin was tanned year-round, and he wore corduroy short shorts and Sperry Top-Siders. The collars of his Izod shirts were always crisply turned up. Chad was cute, smart, rich, and funny. Buh-*bam*.

Chad walked up to me one day after class and said hello. I said hello back. He proceeded to look at his shoes and start muttering. I said, "What?" He kept muttering. I said, "What?" again. He looked up at me, his face red. He pushed his bangs—the bangs that flopped perfectly over his right eye—away from his face and blurted out, "You're the smartest girl I ever met! Will you be my girlfriend?"

I smiled and said, "No."

Chad was a cool guy, but I felt there was something missing, you know? It pained me to let him down (as much as a sixth-grade girl with a sense of relationship entitlement could be pained), but it had to be done. He just wasn't everything I was looking for.

Neither was Gary, who bought me 25 Carnation-Grams during our school's Valentine's Day fund-raiser and wrote separate notes for each one. Or Rich, who painted me a picture in art class. Or Kevin, who said a bunch of mean things about me, then later admitted it was because he was trying to get my attention. Or James; or Jason; or Sean, Michael, or Ben. All of these boys were nice, but none of them were *enough*.

As you can see, my dating prospects were pretty good in the sixth grade. They've been on a downward spiral ever since. I guess I didn't know what I had when I had it.

My mom, of course, doesn't understand this. I'm the youngest of six kids, and my mom was forty-two when I was born. This was back when having kids at forty-two wasn't cool. It certainly wasn't safe, and my mom reminds me of this often. As it is, we have a huge generation gap between us. She's now eighty-six years old and can't for her life figure out why I'm still single.

My mom's story is something you'd expect from someone who got married in the 1950s. She met my dad in college, stalked him at a few basketball games, went to a senior banquet, and he popped the question. They got married, started out dirt poor, built a life together, started having kids, became dirt poor again, and before they knew it, they had fifty years together.

"I don't know why it's so difficult for you," she tells me with a frown. "When I met your dad, I just *knew*." Of course, she conveniently omits the fact that my dad wouldn't even date her at first. She was from Connecticut; he was from a small farm town in northern Minnesota. She arrived as the new girl on their Chicago campus with her powdered face, red lips, and kitten heels. My dad was convinced she was unsaved and didn't give her a second look except to hope that she would attend the next citywide revival and meet the Lord. Her friend did the requisite reconnaissance to determine my dad's misgivings, and within a week my mom was makeup-free and looking substantially more spiritual and demure. With that minor issue resolved, her road to the altar was blissfully unencumbered.

I, on the other hand, have a different story. Sixth-grade conquests notwithstanding, my dating history has had more downs than ups. Okay, if I'm being honest, it's not really the ups or downs but the dry, desolate, winding desert highways that crisscross my dating atlas.

It's not that I didn't want to get married. As I said in the beginning, I always assumed I would. It's more that I didn't even think about it; it wasn't on my radar. Mind you, I grew up in a home that modeled a good marriage. As a child, I played house. I pushed my dolls in their stroller and read them bedtime stories. I bullied the neighbor boy into marrying me many times and personally superintended count-less weddings between Barbie and Ken before they drove off in their Corvette (belonging to the neighbor girls; my parents would never have caved in to buying something so ridiculous when there are still people in the world without Bibles) toward Happily Ever After. I saw good marriages at church and within my extended family. I went to youth group, youth conferences, and family camp. I fell in love with every male camp counselor I met.

But after rejecting all my potential boyfriends in sixth grade and fixing my eyes instead on attending Yale University, I became jaded.

I'll never forget a certain day in eighth grade. It was Occupation Day at school, and we were supposed to dress as what we wanted to be when we grew up. I can't even remember what I wore, but boy, do I remember my friend Lori's costume. Lori was the eldest of seven children in a Mormon family. She lived in our neighborhood a few doors down from me, was one of my best friends, and was pretty much the sweetest girl on the planet. She walked into school that day dressed in a wedding gown. The class burst into laughter, and I was embarrassed for her. I was also embarrassed *by* her. Her biggest aspiration was to be a bride? a wife? maybe even a mom? Poor thing.

I look back on that day with a fair measure of regret. How sad that I not only didn't esteem marriage, but I mocked the girl who did.

I had little time for regrets back then, of course, because at the same time my childhood assumptions around boys and babies were fading, I was being delivered a solid script for my own potential on every other level. I was a first-rate overachiever, and there's nothing the California public schools in the '80s loved more than a female overachiever. My teachers told me I could be anything I wanted to be. They saw me as a leader, and I quickly outpaced my male counterparts in reading, writing, and languages. By high school, I was unstoppable. I started school clubs and joined others. I wrote award-winning essays. I competed in debate. My Government teacher told me I'd someday be a senator. My English teacher wrote in my yearbook that she expected a Nobel Prize out of me. My private flute teacher hoped to see me solo with a symphony.

I dared to believe them.

I stood by, as many of my female teachers, fueled by the feminist gains of the '60s and '70s, dumped their husbands and went back to college for more graduate work. They traveled to Europe, went on archaeological digs, wrote novels, and met in packs after work to drink wine, share their successes, and dream their dreams. There was something intoxicating about witnessing their sense of freedom and *joie de vivre*.

Sadly, as I immersed myself in girl power at school, I received little at church and beyond to counter it. Most of the well-meaning couples in my parents' circle saw no reason to question my trajectory toward worldly success; many of them outright supported it. I was told, as I finished high school and (naturally—why else would I be taking AP Physics?) considered college, to focus on my education and career. Here are a few of the mantras I commonly received—see if any of them sound familiar:

> "Make sure you can support yourself; it's a tough world out there!"
>
> "You're so smart; you don't want to waste your intelligence [implied: by getting married too soon]."
>
> "We're expecting big things from you."
>
> "You have your whole life ahead of you—have fun while you can!"
>
> "Relax; marriage will happen when it happens."
>
> "I wish I'd had all the opportunities you have."

At the time, I didn't think any of these statements were weird. I just figured everyone was happy and had hopes and dreams for me, and I appreciated that. But something bigger was going on. It's something that marks my generation—generation X—and now the generation behind me—generation Y, the millennials.

What I've learned only recently is that all of this opportunity came at a tremendous cost. You see, Xers and millennials are the product of the largest divorce generation in history (yeah, I'm talking about you, Boomers). It's obvious how clueless I was even with my stable background, and here my peers were growing up in broken homes. Many of them grew up without dads. Even more were latch-key kids because their moms returned to the workforce, leaving them home alone for long stretches of time after school and on weekends. While this experience gave me some pretty killer Pac-Man skills and expert knowledge of *The Love Boat* and *Eight is Enough* (I love you, Ralph Macchio!), it didn't make for a cookie-cutter, *Leave It to Beaver* family story.

Take this for what it's worth, older generations: I don't blame you entirely. As you'll see later on, there's plenty that younger folks do to mess up our paths to the altar. I just think it's important to note that when I think back to what I learned about marriage, especially in junior high and high school, I hear only crickets. I can't remember getting a decent narrative about marriage, even though I was in circles of folks who would've, if asked, said it was a good thing.

So if most of my peers had the same general experience, where did this leave us? For too many, it cast a dim view of marriage and family. As a result, a big chunk of our generation, as much as we hate to admit it, is pretty afraid of marriage. We're afraid of getting there, being there, and perhaps most of all, failing at it once we've arrived.

But wait. Between 93 percent and 96 percent of young adults today want to be married.[1] Even more surprising, almost the same percentage is confident that they someday will be. Marriage is still an ideal held by most. It's seen as valuable and normative. And for Christians especially, there's the sense that it'll just *happen*.

But marriage doesn't just happen. Not anymore. Oh sure, there are still couples who meet in college and marry at twenty-one. There are those who find one another at church or work or through a fortuitous setup by family or friends. There are even the scriptworthy stories of those who locked eyes across a room at a party neither had planned to attend, or they were both sent as missionaries to the same remote village in Ecuador. Or perhaps they were trapped in an elevator together or got their orders mixed up at Starbucks. The point is, these stories happen, and praise the Lord they do. But no one is guaranteed such a story, and in a culture that's becoming increasingly "meh" about marriage, I've become more convinced that those who get married young and have marriages go the distance are most often those who have prayed, prepared, and been proactive about their path to the altar.

Gone are the days of *Little House on the Prairie*, when a young single man (a handsome farmer with a sharp wit and the ability to butcher a hog, repair a wagon, and whittle decorative items from wood—yeah, I've read those Christian romances) would attend a box social after church, bid on a single girl's lunch basket, and marry her a few months later. Gone also are the days such as those when my mom grew up—an era when getting married was top of mind for most. It was the next item on life's to-do list after finishing some schooling and maybe serving in a war.

For those generations, not moving toward marriage in a timely and intentional manner prompted questions. That farmer had to have a pretty good reason if he wasn't searching for a wife. If he boarded at a hotel or with a family, it usually wasn't for long. That soldier returned from war, not to take art history classes or teach snowboarding part-time or play video games, but to get a job, find a wife, and start a family.

Similarly, my mom finished college, but marriage was a next step. It was always a priority. It was talked about, planned for, and expected. She didn't mess around when she spotted my dad; she got busy. Her parents stepped in; her friends supported her. My dad was like-minded when it came to marriage, so it was completely natural for them to get to know one another for the purpose of determining if they would be a good marriage match.

What about me? I can count on one hand the people who talked to me about marriage in my twenties. That number's risen in recent years, but only because I've (usually awkwardly and sometimes belligerently) forced the conversation. Not even when I started working for Focus on the Family, the world's largest organization dedicated to helping marriages and families thrive, did anyone get up in my grill about marriage—at least not at first.

Nope, I was the single career girl with promising talent and time in the evenings to work late while my coworkers went home to their families. As a member of Focus's media relations team, I served as a spokesperson for the ministry, yet not once did anyone ask me why I had no family of my own to focus on.

It took me years to discover that, despite immersing myself in a career devoted to the importance of family, I was seriously ignorant about the subject. You may be too. If so, it's not too late to catch the vision of God's purpose for family, especially if you're hoping (or flat-out assuming) family is part of your future. Let's begin with a little Marriage 101.

# CHAPTER 2
# WHAT'S THE BIG DEAL ABOUT MARRIAGE?

I had just given a talk on relationships and dating to about 150 college students at a camp in the Colorado Rockies. My talk was followed by a question-and-answer time, but, as is usually the case with this subject, many students were too embarrassed to ask a question in front of a room full of their peers, so they sought me out afterward to privately share their stories and get advice.

A line of about twenty students snaked before me. First up was a cheerful-looking guy who shuffled forward shyly and thanked me for my message that evening. He then inhaled sharply and began with something I'm convinced I've now heard about a hundred times.

"Okay, I'm not anywhere close to getting married—in fact, I hardly ever think about it—but I was just wondering ..."

Bless his heart.

It still surprises me how little some young adults think about marriage. Oh, I know it's in the back of their minds somewhere, but when they say the word, it's like a toy they're taking out of the box for the first time on Christmas morning. It's a distant term—almost foreign. They talk of marriage apologetically, as though they've been caught in an illicit act, like bringing up the subject is entirely inappropriate, but they just can't help it.

Even though young adults (and for the most part, I'm talking about twentysomethings here) absolutely see marriage *somewhere* in their future, few I talk with seem to see it as an option for their *immediate* future. The general consensus is, "Yeah, I'm going to get married someday, but after I've lived a little, had some fun, and generally gotten my life together."

What they're saying is that they're waiting to marry until they grow up. The problem is, they *are* grown, but they seem to be the only ones who don't know it.

My sister's father-in-law grew up during the Depression on a farm in Minnesota, the eldest of seven children. The family struggled daily to make ends meet.

His mother died when he was only fourteen years old, and his father died tragically seven months later. He quit school after eighth grade to help with the farm and the younger children, and he took over operation of the farm several years later. He never finished school, nor did he travel the world, play sports, hang out with friends, or spend time "finding himself." He grew up. Too fast, of course, but you get my point. He worked that farm for the next sixty years. He married, raised a family, served at church, and lived a full life. He had no regrets, because he hadn't wasted any time.

The problem with waiting to get your life in order before considering marriage is that you really have no idea when your life *will* be in order, if ever. I mean, in this culture of wanting more and expecting more, it seems that very few people "arrive" anymore. Yet we're determined to do things on our terms and our timeline with no messiness or inconvenience. We insist on scripting our stories to suit our hyper-detailed preferences and timelines. Usually this has us going to extremes, especially in regard to marriage and family. We either piddle around, thinking we have all the time in the world, or we shut everything else out and dive headlong into a path of self-defined success and self-improvement, refusing to take on family until our ducks are in the proverbial row.

You know what that gets you? It gets you my story—waking up at thirty and discovering you're still single and thinking it all should've been easier than this.

Even with cautionary tales like myself aplenty, most singles don't like to talk about marriage or their desire for it. Wanting marriage—ironically, even praying for it—is often equated with not trusting God or taking matters into our own hands. If God wants us to be married, he'll get us married, right? Don't we have better things to do—serving at church, going on mission trips, building a career, and being generally happy about our present circumstances? We don't want to come across as grumpy or ungrateful. Shoot, it's not as if we're starving in a third-world country or in prison somewhere because of our faith or trapped in a loveless marriage or any number of worst-case scenarios.

I'm not saying we shouldn't trust God with our present circumstances. We should. Nor am I saying that thoughts of getting hitched should consume every waking moment. Far from it. What I am saying is that in all our efforts to (rightly) affirm single adults, we've (wrongly) made very little of marriage.

It's too bad Martha Stewart doesn't have a marriage show. Smiling couples could rhapsodize about the joys of married life while standing in an immaculate kitchen or craft room making pumpkin bisque, stringing pinecones, folding paper lanterns, or setting party tables in any number of themes. Martha would then saunter over in her robin's-egg-blue cashmere sweater set, smile knowingly at them, and affirm their heartwarming stories and successes by proclaiming, "It's a good thing."

Well, we don't need Martha Stewart to say that—God already has.

The fact is, God is a big fan of marriage. Not only is he a fan of marriage in general, but he's a big fan of *your* marriage, even if it hasn't happened yet.

God's still in the business of making good matches.[1] Marriage is part of God's grand design. And most people in the world will be married at some point in their lives. Statistics show that more than 80 percent of people will tie the knot in their lifetimes.[2] That percentage probably includes you.

God's so passionate about marriage that he modeled it after himself. He wants the intimacy of marriage to reflect the intimacy he has with the Son and Holy Spirit. There is oneness there, a communion and perfection of complementary roles. There is communication, submission, and fellowship.

When God made the first man, Adam, it wasn't long before he said, "It is not good that the man should be alone; I will make him a helper fit for him" (Gen. 2:18). Notice he didn't say, "I'm gonna wait around and see how Adam does on his own. I'll let him get some experience under his belt first, then see if it's a good idea to throw a woman into the mix."

No, God was extremely intentional when it came to creating man, woman, and the unique relationship they would share. He didn't just stop in Genesis, either. Yes, the Bible begins with marriage. But it also ends with marriage. The ultimate marriage will happen when Jesus Christ returns for his bride, the church. Marriage on earth between men and women is a reflection of the relationship Christ will have with the universal body of believers whom he's redeemed. This is nothing short of extraordinary. We're getting a small (though imperfect) taste of it now.

So the Bible begins with marriage and ends with marriage. But it also talks a lot about marriage in between. Marriage is a biblical norm. You see good marriages in Scripture and you see bad marriages. You see patterns of faithfulness, purity, and devotion to God, but you also see patterns of betrayal, divorce, adultery, polygamy, interfaith marriage, marriage for political purposes, and more.

Even though humans have messed up marriage in every generation throughout history, that doesn't change what marriage is. Marriage is a covenant, a sacrament, a reflection of Christ and his bride, the church. It's an institution for one man and one woman for one lifetime. The definition of marriage isn't determined by popular opinion; it was delivered by God in the garden, then affirmed by Jesus in the New Testament. Consider these words from Matthew 19:4–6: "He answered, 'Have you not read that he who created them from the beginning made them male and female, and said, "Therefore a man shall leave his father and his mother and hold fast to his wife, and the two shall become one flesh"? So they are no longer two but one flesh. What therefore God has joined together, let not man separate.'" There's a lot to be said for marriage and about marriage in Scripture. We'd be wise to pay attention.

Marriage also has a bunch of benefits. Marriage polishes our edges. The fancy word for this is sanctification. Pastor Gary Thomas says that marriage isn't meant to make us happy but holy.[3] How many of us sit around and ask how we can be holier? Not me. (I do, however, ask myself how *others* can be holier!) Marriage accomplishes this naturally. If you're going to have a successful marriage, be prepared to get over yourself. Fast. And if you have kids—goodness, watch out. That's where selfishness truly goes to die. My friend Kara once told me, "I never knew how selfish I was until I got married, and I never knew how angry I was until I had kids." Truth.

But there's great companionship in marriage too. Newsflash! Marriage can actually be fun. Most people dream of that person who will walk through life with them. The one who will make memories with them, share hobbies, go on trips, celebrate holidays, dream big, raise a family, set up a home, and ultimately grow old with them. We are created for relationship. In a culture that throws away relationships with Friday's trash, it's easy to lose sight of this. Don't. Sure, many of you don't have family photo albums that span decades. At some point, Dad walked out, or your parents calmly divvied up possessions and kids like candy and started over in different cities. Maybe your parents were never married. This is far from God's plan. Don't let what you never experienced taint your understanding of what could be.

Marriage generally makes people healthier. Now, don't get all defensive. I can already hear some of you singles shouting at the page the number of miles you run per week and how you're vegan, never eat sweets, sleep nine hours a night, and drink reverse-osmosis water. Good for you. My point is, studies show that marriage as a general rule makes people live longer. They eat better, watch out for each other, have more positive outlooks, go to the doctor more, and engage in less risky behaviors. University of Chicago sociologist Linda J. Waite focused most of her career on the effects of marriage on various demographics. In her book *The Case for Marriage*, she noted, "The evidence from four decades of research is surprisingly clear: a good marriage is both men's and women's best bet for living a long and healthy life."[4]

While we're talking about health, let's not forget emotional health and maturity. Folks, marriage grows us up. It's the fast track for taking on responsibility, focusing one's career, stewarding time, and being accountable to someone other than yourself. As I said above, once kids enter the picture, the process accelerates even more. Now you have mouths to feed, lives to shape, and little eyes watching your every move. No pressure.

You want to hear another motivation for getting married?

Sex.

I'm serious. For Christians, a desire for sex should be a healthy and honest reason to get married. Because (and it bugs me that I have to remind you) sex apart from marriage is wrong.[5] I'm not sure where we lost sight of this, but I'm sad that we have. Rates of premarital sex and even cohabitation among Christians are climbing.[6] We've separated sex from marriage and are reaping the consequences individually, as a culture, and as the church when we grapple with unplanned pregnancies, sexually transmitted diseases, broken hearts, broken families, divorce, poverty, and more.[7]

Not waiting for sex is a symptom of ultimately not trusting God. I remember hearing about a guy who approached his pastor and boldly announced, "I'm giving sex to God until I'm twenty-five. He'd better get me married by then, because if he doesn't, I'm gonna do things my way. Because you know what? I'm sure as heck not gonna be a virgin at thirty years old."

Cue lightning bolt. Yikes.

There's audacity in that statement, to be sure, but there's also fear. This guy was afraid to put his heart, his body, and his future in God's hands. But we all know (or we lie and say we do) that being in God's hands is exactly where we and our futures should be.

But trusting is so hard. Especially when we are eager to believe lies—lies that we think will deliver the happiness we so desperately long for.

One of these lies is that if you go to your grave not having had sex, you're somehow an incomplete person. We've given sex far too much power in our culture and in our individual lives. We've made it the be-all, end-all definition of masculinity and femininity. We've made it the rite of passage to adulthood.

This is so bogus. Kids are having sex these days, for crying out loud. Masculinity, femininity, and all the other inherent qualities of male and female are so much more than a sexual act. But we don't believe it, so we chuck out the window everything we say we believe in favor of testing the waters. We assume we must be missing something big. We don't preach truth to ourselves; we don't exercise strength in the face of temptation (nor do we bother to flee temptation); we don't swim against the cultural tide.

We cave.

We want to keep our options open. We want to have fun. Some of us even want to hold off on growing up. Yet we still want sex.

But in God's book, sex and marriage go hand in hand. So if you want sex and you want to honor God, start considering marriage.

If you've already had sex, it's not too late to start over. Sure, you'll have some tough stuff to walk through as you process your past, but assuming you're a failure or unfit to marry won't get you anywhere. Neither will chanting to yourself that "sex is bad, sex is dirty"—because it's not. Sex is fun. Sex is pleasurable. Sex creates a beautiful bond between two people.

Knowing this, don't you want those memories and that unique intimacy to be with someone who's committed his or her entire being to you? By God's grace, you can have that. I've never had one married person tell me they wish they'd had more sex with more partners before tying the knot. I've heard many married people say they wish they'd waited.

Confess your sin before God and others, take responsibility for your previous decisions, get accountability for the road ahead from godly, trusted people, and walk forward in confidence. God is eager to lavish forgiveness, grace, and fresh starts on those who humbly repent and ask for them.

In light of this, there's obviously nothing wrong with wanting sex, so why are we all so weird about saying so? Sure, you probably shouldn't ask a girl out with, "I'm auditioning potential wives so I can get some sex before I'm dead." That won't get you far. But as you think about marriage (and your sex drive, which isn't hard to do), consider the fact that God made sex and is all for it. Within marriage.

And lest you wonder if God wants to cheat you out of marriage (and sex), here's the thing: marriage is for most people! I mean, c'mon. Aside from the Bible making much out of marriage in general, it's also pretty obvious that marriage is the relational default; it's the foundation of the family and society, both in ancient times and today. Every culture has within it a construct of marriage[8], and most of us are called to marriage.

Some of you aren't and that's perfectly fine. Paul had great things to say about those who are called to singleness, or celibate service. It's a unique calling and one that should be celebrated. But it's pretty rare, and those who are called to it generally know they are. They should also be comfortable with that calling. Those who are truly called to a life of celibate service generally don't struggle overwhelmingly with their sex drive nor do they feel any sense of being less in God's eyes. Because they're not. Most singles in this camp have a very clear vision of how God wants to use them, and it generally involves a calling that is better lived out without a spouse and kids.

Let's not confuse this, though, with the assumption many have that marriage can wait. This isn't a true call to singleness; instead, it's a selfish desire to accomplish things (usually big things) that being married will in some way hinder or delay. I get this a lot from single women. They talk to me of their desire for marriage, but it's always couched in terms of "when I'm good and ready." Usually this means that the woman plans to finish advanced degrees and/or do "big things for God." First of all, not everyone is called to dig wells in Africa or serve in the US Senate. Second, most of those types of callings work just fine for a married couple. Ladies, consider: God is big. He's all-knowing and all-powerful. He knows how to make your life matter. The fact that he created you means you matter. Don't diss being a wife and mother in favor of chasing after something that seems sexy and significant. Be open to what God has for you, and let *him* add the excitement.

Men approach this assumption a different way. Many men dread marriage. They see it as a sort of end, stifling everything they're free to do while single and responsible for no one but themselves. Guys see a clock ticking, and it's a race to the finish to see who can maximize experiences and squeeze the most out of life before the drudgery of bills and babies sets in. It's true that marriage forces you to give up a few things. My brother-in-law traded in his tricked-out BMW for a minivan after marrying my sister and accumulating a kid or two. He could no longer fly to Hawaii at the drop of a hat or go to a game with his buddies or eat hot wings every night of the week. His life changed, but he wouldn't trade it for the world. Sure, sometimes it's hard and he pines for his bachelorhood, but overall, he knows he made the right choice.

Remember, all of us are called to a season of singleness. Some seasons will be longer than others (don't I know it), but if you're meant to be married, you should anticipate and prepare for that season, not expect it to hit you like the flu. Marriage is too important to be treated haphazardly or as one of life's ancillary endeavors.

So let me be frank. If you're not called to singleness, you're called to marriage. Knowing this should not be terrifying, but freeing. It should give you a sense of direction. It should motivate you to consider the future and weigh your current actions in light of that future. It should give you hope.

I'm often asked if marriage (or the pursuit of marriage) can become an idol. Well, I guess so. An idol is anything that takes God's rightful place in our lives and removes our focus from him, and that's not good. If we treat marriage as something we're owed—and not getting it on our terms and timeline makes us bitter, crazy, or all-around ungrateful—we need a major heart check. It also doesn't help in the attractiveness department. Being open and honest about a desire for marriage is attractive; dissolving into a puddle of tears every time it's mentioned is not.

But for most people, the honest desire for and intentional pursuit of marriage brings good fruit. It's a God-given desire and in alignment with his will. God's a big fan of marriage, folks. Remember, he designed it.

So when's the time to start thinking about marriage? It's now. I tell parents of young children that if they haven't started casting a vision for marriage in their homes, they're already behind. It's never too early to show your babies what a good marriage looks like. It's never wrong to teach a young boy the proper way to treat a woman. Little girls should know that wives and mommies have a sacred calling that may someday be theirs. It all matters.

Likewise, if you're twenty, don't relegate marriage to the distant future. Yes, the average age of first marriage has climbed. In 1960, it was age twenty for women and twenty-two for men. Those numbers have now shot up to twenty-six and twenty-nine.[9] But there's little evidence that this is overall a good thing. Instead, it's leading to delays in maturity, job success, and childbearing. It's also making books like this necessary, because there's a lot of hand-wringing among singles who wonder if they missed their window and were left behind when the marriage train pulled out of the station.

I'm not trying to create a panic. I'm not saying you need to run out right now and grab the first guy or girl you see. I'm just asking you to consider marriage. Start praying about it. Cultivate an active desire for it in your heart. Let others know that you're open to it. And honor it, even as a single person.

Hebrews 13:4 says, "Let marriage be held in honor among all." That includes those who aren't married yet and those who may never get married. Follow God's example and have a high view of marriage. Our churches, our culture, and our families desperately need it.

Similarly, if you're thirty or older, don't give up on the idea of marriage. I haven't. You simply don't know what God has in store for your future. It may not be the story you expected, but God never drops the ball. He's never late, and he's not capricious. Wait for your story to unfold, and do your part in crafting it. (More on that later.) In the meantime, let's go inside our heads and figure out how we got kind of messed up in our relationship thinking.

# CHAPTER 3
# DITCH THE
# HOLLYWOOD SCRIPT

Okay, I'll admit it—I'm occasionally a little too into pop culture. I know some (maybe more than some) hip-hop lyrics, follow Lady Gaga and Conan O'Brien on Twitter, and catch up on celebrity magazines when I fly. I envy Kate Middleton's hair, Jennifer Lopez's skin, and Kate Winslet's wardrobe (and accent, eyes, and general proximity to Colin Firth). Not surprisingly, the world of TV, music, magazines, and movies has had a gradual, subtle, yet undeniable effect on me over the years. Take for example the following nuggets of wisdom I've gleaned from the entertainment and ad industries:

- If you wait long enough, the guy who sees you as just a friend will eventually come to his senses and fall in love with you (*Some Kind of Wonderful*)
- The best way to get a man to love you is to stalk him relentlessly (Lady Gaga's "Paparazzi")

- Crocs look good on everyone (Crocs ad campaigns)
- All men are misogynistic jerks (Taio Cruz's "Break Your Heart")
- The angrier and crazier you are, the more attractive you are (*Gossip Girl*, *Cruel Intentions*, any daytime soap opera)
- The best doctors are drug-addicted narcissists with no bedside manner whatsoever (*House*)
- You can become a professional athlete in just six steps (eHow.com)
- If you absolutely loathe a guy, your chances of someday marrying him increase exponentially (*You've Got Mail*, *Bridget Jones's Diary*, *Life as We Know It*, and every other movie loosely based on *Pride and Prejudice*)
- Someday your prince *will* come (hello, Disney, you're killing us)

The truth is, every sentiment shared above is total garbage. Yet how many of us catch ourselves spouting (or worse, demonstrating) variations of these pop-culture adages from time to time in our thoughts, assumptions, and actions?

Nowhere is this more evident than in the way we approach dating and relationships. And by "we," sadly, I'm talking about Christians.

Consider the way you see dating done in your church, at your Christian college, and among your friends. You probably don't see much difference between the way relationships are done there and in the world at large. It's the same me-centered, cowardly approach to dating that allows one to keep his or her options open and treat the other person like a commodity.

Why is this?

I'd argue it's because we've been duped. We've been lulled into believing that marriage—and the process of getting there—is nothing more than one big Hollywood plotline.

You know how it goes. Guy meets girl, and one of two things happens: they either fall in love at first sight (they just *know*), or they immediately hate each other. About ninety minutes and a spectacular series of plot twists later, they overcome unbelievable odds and end up together. Despite having nothing in common, too much in common, little support from family and friends, even less time spent together, devastating pasts, and enough baggage to weigh down a 747, the couple makes it work.

Or maybe they just make out. And have sex, of course. You can't fit everything in that hour and a half. But the assumption is, this thing will go on forever. It's destined to be. From now on, it'll be easy.

Remember Jerry Maguire? He tearfully told Dorothy Boyd, "You. Complete. Me." She believed him. We assume they got married and sailed through the challenges of his historic narcissism, her life as a single parent, their rocky employment history, and a host of other pretty big dysfunctions. We don't know, because the movie ended with them acting as if none of it mattered.

Most of the relationships I've lived in my head follow a similar script. I meet a guy who is seemingly immune to my beauty and ignorant of my brilliance. He is somehow still single despite being devastatingly handsome, rich, successful, smart, and outrageously witty. This is, I decide, because he has (unbeknownst to him) been saved for me. And his number is about to be called.

None of these daydream-inspired relationships panned out for me, primarily because they didn't exist. Nor did the guys, for that matter, but let's not split hairs. I've witnessed a number of singles approach dating and the path to marriage with a similar script running through their heads. What you see as a result is a bunch of Christian singles serial dating, dating with no direction, dating indefinitely, non-dating (I'll define that later), dating without boundaries or a blueprint for purity, or not dating at all.

Guys and girls have different aspects of the Hollywood trap that uniquely trip them up. Let's look at a few examples, starting with the guys.

## I WANT A SUPERMODEL WHO WRITES BIBLE STUDIES

Guys, you're attracted to hotness. I get it. And on some level, it's not a bad thing. You're wired to notice and appreciate beauty. Wonderful. But things get dicey when your Hollywood Romance Radar starts tracking the truly unattainable.

I've seen it a bunch of times. A guy waits and waits … and waits … to date because what he's looking for, he's not finding.

What's he looking for? He's looking for an ideal. And usually, this starts with the physical. We all know that guys see it as a badge of honor to be able to date the prettiest girl in their acquaintance. Now, there's nothing wrong with a girl being pretty or a guy wanting to date a pretty girl. Pretty girls deserve dates and husbands too. But if physical attraction is a guy's common denominator and his standard of physical attraction is off the charts, he's gonna be single for a long time.

Scott Croft, one of our writers at Boundless, wrote a piece several years ago that completely slayed me. It was the first time I had ever heard a guy call out another guy on this issue. It was refreshing. And a little vindicating.

Scott wrote about a guy who approached him to complain about the lack of quality single women in his sphere. He bemoaned the fact that he couldn't meet any "tens," no matter how hard he tried.

Scott's response? "But, brother, look at yourself. You're like a six."[1]

I'd love to hear from that guy now. Those were frank words, to be sure, but they no doubt jolted that guy out of his fantasy world, provided he was even a smidge teachable.

Why do guys fall prey to this? Some of it is their own arrogance, but some of it can be blamed on Hollywood. Look at all the men on TV and in films who are unattractive, bumbling idiots—or worse, complete jerks—yet they defy the odds by scoring hot women who overlook all their faults and (eventually, if not right away) see them for their true, manly selves.

Of course, Christian guys don't fall for this, right?

Well, yeah, many of them do.

But Christian guys take it a step further. Christian guys want it all. Of course they want a beautiful girl; that's who they'll ask out. And they'll generally hold out until they find her. But they know that beauty will only take a relationship so far. So for the girl to be marriage material, she needs to have a bunch of other qualities too.

She needs to be smart.

And funny (or even better, think *he's* funny).

She needs to be laid back. And not too much drama. And sweet.

And then if she leads worship at church or teaches Sunday school, even better. And she should cook and have a cute apartment. And be debt free. You know, a true Proverbs 31 woman. Bonus points if she loves orphans, fair trade coffee, and football.

Guys, all I'm saying is that, for all the ways women are controlling (and we are), this is one area where you take the cake. I'm exaggerating the above, of course, and I've met a number of Christian guys who defy this stereotype, but still. I've met (and even dated) enough of this type to merit a mention of it.

If finding someone superhot is no guarantee of relational success, why is it such a priority for you? I'm always saddened when I hear of yet another Jennifer Aniston– or Scarlett Johansson–type breakup. Why can't those girls find love? Why aren't their boyfriends desperate to hold on to them? I guess famous actresses and supermodels get dumped too.

Most guys won't admit they're looking for flat-out hotness, and few are actually delusional enough to think they'll marry a supermodel. But most, when asked what makes or breaks a decision to ask a girl out, will cite chemistry as a major factor.

Chemistry is a safer, saner, and sometimes more spiritual way of saying you're looking for hotness. Yet if you ask most married guys what the most important qualities in their wives are, attractiveness (or even chemistry) rarely makes the list. There's something about being married to a person that brings out what's truly important.

## I WANT TO RISK LITTLE, BUT WIN BIG

The other way Hollywood calls to men has to do with significance. All of us want to matter, but men need to be needed. They need to be part of something bigger than themselves. They need to join a story, an adventure. This is a good thing; it's what prompts men to lead, to get dirty, to sacrifice—even to die. It's what sends men to war. It's why men scuttled women and children onto lifeboats as the *Titanic* sank beneath them. It caused them to throw their bodies in front of their wives and girlfriends in 2012's theater shooting in Aurora, Colorado.

Hollywood knows a good thing when it sees it. Enter the blockbuster action movie. And the ever-growing superhero franchises. The film industry knows how to get men to drop twelve bucks and sit in a darkened theater for two hours. The problem is, more and more men are settling for watching a story unfold before their eyes instead of being part of one. Men are starting to live their adventures through others, even if those others are fictitious. Whether movies, TV shows, video games, or another virtual-reality pursuit, these hobbies, though harmless in and of themselves, are starting to suck major time, attention, and energy from the very men we need to be fighting valiantly in a culture that has very real threats and missions.

When I've asked my guy friends why they fall prey to this, their answer is honest, but sad: they want to win but want to risk little.

My friend told me about a guy in her church who went to a local water park on a hot summer day. After spending a day on the slides, he was in the dressing room changing. As he was collecting his things, he saw a man in the corner of the room. On the bench beside him was a backpack, the zipper open. The man adjusted the backpack several times, but didn't put anything in it or take anything out of it. Church Guy looked around the room and saw a small boy changing out of his swimsuit directly in line of the backpack. He now noticed that a couple of the other men in the room were looking toward the backpack, but none made a move. Everyone went about his business, though most looked uncomfortable. Some picked up their things and left the building.

At this point, so did the backpack man. He zipped his pack, slung it on his shoulder, and slipped quietly out the door of the men's locker room. In a split-second decision, Church Guy followed him.

The man was headed toward the parking lot and as soon as he saw Church Guy on his heels, he began to run. Church Guy ran after him. Breaking into a full sprint, Church Guy tackled the man with the backpack in the middle of the parking lot as parkgoers looked on. He ripped the backpack off the guy and opened it. Inside was a small video camera. The man had been filming small boys in the changing room and had been there for a while. Others had seen it or at least suspected something. Only Church Guy actually did anything.

That's a man.

Guys, it's time to be men. To stop settling for nonsense. It's time to be different—to buck a culture of low expectations and lackadaisical, passive playacting and get in the game. You don't have to be a bodybuilder, gunslinger, or linebacker to be a man; you do have to be wise, pay attention, and act at the appropriate time. Rarely will you be called to tackle a pedophile in a parking lot. But there are many battles to be fought each day that need men of God to fight them. Battles in your family, your church, our culture—even in your own mind and heart. Don't give up. Don't pop in a Blu-ray and act as if you're part of the movie. Live your own story—a real one with a real ending and a real victory. We need you.

## I WANT A PROJECT TO WORK ON

Okay, ladies, now it's your turn. Because for as much as that guy is battling fake bad guys and pining for an airbrushed, yet amazingly talented princess to rescue and woo with his considerable charm, you have to admit that we women are prone to reading the script wrong too.

In the same movies I talked about above—the ones with the stupid or unenlightened guys—who is it that has to step in and save them from themselves and ultimately save the day?

Yeah, it's the women. Most of the time, the woman has sworn off love altogether and is focusing on her high-powered career, macrobiotic diet, and Jimmy Choo shoe collection. But then some guy, a bona fide project, stumbles into her life and, against her will, she falls in love with him.

This is not acceptable, of course, because he needs a considerable amount of work. He's usually jobless, directionless, an alcoholic, clinically depressed, a serial womanizer, or worse. But that's okay. She'll fix him.

Fixing him involves bringing all of her girlfriends on the scene, usually at an expensive restaurant or in a vinyasa yoga class or at a wine bar. They talk. They weigh his faults against his merits (of which they inevitably find some). They devise a plan for making this happen and somehow discover that beneath this lad's ne'er-do-well reputation lies an Ivy League grad with a houseboat, an almost-finished bestselling novel, connections to the Kennedys, and nothing more than an existential crisis, wounded heart, or a few daddy issues tripping him up.

Well, you know what? I've dated projects, and they never turned out to be diamonds in the rough. They turned out to be projects. What I *didn't* see was what I got. So much for the Hollywood make-over miracle.

## I WANT A PRINCE (BECAUSE I'M A PRINCESS)

On the other end of the spectrum, some women, in the spirit of not settling, seem perpetually unwilling to date and marry perfectly normal, average guys. Remember me in the sixth grade? Oh, and most of my twenties?

Blame it on my days in church youth group. Maybe you remember it too—a night when the girls and guys were split up for discussion and a well-meaning pastor or layperson gave a lengthy talk on purity or waiting for the One. (My friend's dad actually gave the talk at her youth group. Now there's a scar that won't heal. Ever.)

That's when it happened. The leader passed out notebook paper and a pen to each girl, and we were told to write down the qualities we most wanted in a husband. All of them. Nothing was too big, because "nothing's too big for God."

I think I numbered my page from one to fifty. I wasn't going to be cheated on this one. I wrote "Christian" on the top, because I wanted God to know I was serious. I also had some excellent character qualities listed. But by numbers forty through fifty, I was asking for everything from a specific height range to hair color.

When everyone finished scribbling, our leader prayed over our lists. We were then told to take our list home, tape it to our bathroom mirror, and continue praying for the days, weeks, months, and years between then and when we would inevitably meet our prince.

That's what we called him. Our prince. And we were princesses. God's princesses. His daughters, who deserved nothing less than God's best. And while we were determining God's best, the message was clear: *don't settle for anything less.*

Ladies, we've gone nuts.

Of course God wants us to marry a great guy. Of course he wants us to find someone who loves us, treats us right, and maybe even makes our heart beat a little faster. He certainly wants someone whose calling we can join, a man with whom we can serve God with effectiveness and joy.

But while I'm all for understanding our worth in God's eyes, remember that we're not perfect prima donnas who deserve the best and nothing less. On the contrary, we're sinners who will someday marry other sinners. God has a plan for our future marriages, and it's not to fulfill all our dreams or give us a storybook ending. His goal is to work out his purposes and glorify himself.

There are a lot of women who tell me their dreams of marrying a famous preacher or author. They want to marry "a guy like John Piper." You know what? John Piper wasn't John Piper when he was twenty-three years old. Who he is today is a result of a lot of Christ's work in his life. I often wonder if having access to online sermons and podcasts has done us a disservice, because it's made all of the outliers available to us. It's made us women think that everyone marries a John Piper or Andy Stanley or Francis Chan.

But not everyone does. Most women marry Justin the plumber who loves Jesus and serves in his church's children's ministry. Or Mike the accountant who volunteers his time keeping a local mission agency's books in order. Or Doug the teacher who's leading a Bible study for his neighbors. Who will marry these guys? Perhaps you will.

But what about Evan the graphic designer who stumbles into church late and doesn't really know anyone but is at least there most weeks (when he's not skiing or sleeping in)? Hold up. I think service is a huge hallmark of maturity. I wouldn't encourage a woman to marry a guy who hasn't found a way to give back to his church or community. Does he have to be up front or the person in charge? No. Does he have to be involved and show commitment and sacrifice? Yes. A thirtysomething guy who only warms a pew for one hour a week has bigger things to work on before marriage, especially when enabled by a generation of women who are overcommitted (not good, either) and picking up the men's slack.

Men and women, the process of dating and moving toward marriage is a lot simpler than we make it out to be. Sure, there has to be romance and mystery and pursuit and the very real working of God in the relationship. But if you're sitting around waiting for a mystical experience where the stars align, fireworks explode, and Puccini plays in the background, you're better off buying tickets to the next blockbuster rom-com.

# CHAPTER 4
# FIVE REASONS YOUR LOVE LIFE IS A DISASTER (OR DOESN'T EXIST)

Okay, so you know you've been messed up by Hollywood. You realize you haven't given marriage a fair shake and suspect you've left the rational, realistic, and serious pursuit of a spouse on the back burner. Instead, you've waited for your Ideal List Man or Ideal List Woman to show up, but he or she hasn't and you're still single.

No biggie. All that's left to do is watch a little less TV and sign up for a marriage class at church, right? Surely that'll do the trick?

Not so fast.

Sorry to disappoint, but while getting our heads out of Hollywood is a great start, there are actually bigger and sneakier traps we've fallen into when it comes to finding love. And—get this—some of them are being perpetuated by (gasp!) the churches we attend and the Christian circles we run in. Yeah, I said it.

In fact, I'm going to say right here that after years of hearing lame-o dating stories (and even more lame-o breakup stories) coupled with the collective whining of the tragically lovelorn, I've come up with what I feel are the five biggest reasons most of us have dysfunctional, directionless, or flat-out DOA love lives.

While not an exhaustive list by any means, these are the biggies—the ones that trip us up over and over again. These are the ones that are keeping us single. And lest you think I sit on my high horse and wag a finger, let me assure you, I've been guilty of all five. Some at the same time, even. So much for moral superiority.

So here we go. The five reasons your love life is a disaster (or doesn't exist).

## REASON NUMBER ONE: YOU'RE WAITING FOR "THE ONE"

Two-thirds of Americans believe in soul mates or this concept of "the One."[1] This is the idea that there's one ideal match for you in the world, and he or she is "out there" somewhere. It's the person you're most compatible with, who'll complete you, and who has been reserved (by God, fate, or the universe, depending on your worldview) exclusively for you.

The problem is, we have a bunch of people expecting a soul mate, but we have a lifetime divorce risk of more than 40 percent (thankfully mitigated by a number of factors, including faith, so don't despair). So if we believe in soul mates but are ditching our marriages, what gives? Why don't the numbers add up? Are we really that bad at picking the supposed loves of our lives?

Personally, I think the idea of the One is completely bogus. It's neither biblical nor practical. And it sets us up for one of two huge potential failures. Let me explain.

On the one hand, waiting for the One leads to relationship paralysis, because how can a person be sure? If that girl is great, but so is this one and so is the one over there, how do you choose? What too many end up doing is not choosing at all. They wait and wait, either for every possible fact and assurance or for an unmistakable gut feeling or a sign. If they're not satisfied with what they're seeing or feeling, they wait. They continue to search or to dabble in relationships or to hold on to a relationship, hoping they'll get the necessary confidence to move ahead. It may never come.

On the other hand, some fall in love, completely intoxicated by the overwhelming amazingness of those they fall in love with. They rush into marriage, each certain they've found the One. *This is who I've been waiting for! It doesn't get better than this!* But at the first bump in the road, that first unwelcome interruption to marital bliss, they pause.

*This shouldn't be happening. Isn't this why I made sure to marry my soul mate?* And by marrying one's soul mate, doesn't that practically guarantee a problem-free marriage? After all, *This person should understand me. Shoot, he or she should read my mind. But now we're fighting. We're seeing things we didn't see before. To be honest, I don't like this person at all right now. Did I make a mistake? Did I not marry my soul mate after all? This isn't working, so the only solution is to start over. Because the One is out there, and I need to find him or her.*

And so they divorce and look for greener pastures. Another marriage becomes a casualty. A statistic.

My friend Motte was looking for the One. In the meantime, he was hanging out with Beth. He and Beth went to church together and were in the same line of work. He enjoyed Beth's company and thought she was attractive. She also had a number of other great qualities. In fact, if he were honest, he would say she was marriage material.

But was she the One?

He took her out a few times and even toyed with the idea of getting serious, but he didn't want to commit. He didn't want to make a mistake. Finally, an older man whom he greatly respected approached him with a question. "What's going on with Beth?" he asked. Taken aback, Motte wasn't sure how to answer. He felt a little defensive, quite frankly. The man was undeterred.

"You need to figure out what you're doing," he continued. "Are you dating her or not? Because if you're not dating her and this is going nowhere, you're wasting her time. If that's the case, you need to let her go." In effect, he told him to fish or cut bait. In other words, Motte needed to pursue Beth with intention or free her to be pursued by someone else—someone who was serious, about her heart and about marriage.

I remember Motte telling me what happened. It was as if in that moment he saw everything clearly, that it was time to choose. Because while there were many wonderful women in his acquaintance, Beth was everything he could ask for, and she was right in front of him. This was a woman he could build his life with.

"I pursued her for marriage," Motte said, "and I didn't look back. The day I married Beth, she became the One. All my other options were eliminated. Now I can spend the rest of my life knowing that she's the one I invest in, the one I love, the one I serve, the one I'll grow old with."

You may be in a similar situation. That girl from church is great, but so is your sister's roommate. And there's the girl you just met. She seems cool. But that girl over there plays guitar. You love the guitar!

Stop the craziness. Know that there are a number of women in the world (we don't know how many, but let's conservatively say hundreds and hundreds) whom you can be attracted to, love, live with, serve with, share a calling with, start a family with, and honor God with.

This should be very freeing. You don't need to find the One. You just need to find one. Of many. And once you cut the clutter, focus on what's important (we'll get to that), and choose, you'll be on your way to a marriage that makes sense and ultimately makes a difference. You'll find *your* one.

## REASON NUMBER TWO: YOU'RE STILL A KID

A while back, I met a guy online. He lived in another state, but I was in a season of attempting to make most relationships work, so I figured a few thousand miles was no obstacle to true love.

This guy was funny. He was verbally quick, witty, and quite smart. He was also cool. Nothing ruffled him. I was smitten. We emailed, texted, and eventually started talking on the phone. As I got to know him, I learned a few things about him. He loved routine. He ran the same route every morning, ate one of two things for breakfast every day, played basketball with the same guys in the same gym, frequented the same takeout joints, and kept the same schedule as best he could. He was stable, as far as I could tell. That's good, right?

But all that stability started to irk me. Not because I thought he should be some sort of reckless madman, but because in everything he did, he took the safe road. He was good at his job. But when I asked him about a promotion that was available and I thought he could easily get, he demurred. He said he liked his current position and didn't want more responsibility. When he shared a dream of seeing new places, I asked him about a move. No, he didn't want to uproot. He liked his small apartment and didn't want to lose it.

Shockingly, this guy eventually decided to travel to Colorado to meet me. For all his laid-back coolness, spending time together revealed a few more things. Like, he didn't want to pay for a hotel room, so I asked one of my pastors if he and his wife would open up their spare room. They did. He stayed for about four days, and (I'm still ashamed every time I say this) with the exception of a couple of Starbucks runs, I paid for pretty much everything we did.

Sure, I'm at fault for letting it happen. But c'mon. After building this guy up in my head, I was stunned to see the way things played out. I couldn't believe it, quite frankly. One night, we decided to go out for dinner. I asked him what he was in the mood for, and he responded, "I don't know. Do you have a gift card for anyplace?"

Folks, I'm not making this up. The sad thing is, I did have a gift card to a local restaurant, and after dinner, I presented it. You think that's bad? Well, I also paid the difference—the remainder of the bill, tip and all. I was so embarrassed and confused, I didn't know what else to do.

Needless to say, that relationship didn't work out, but in reflecting on it, other red flags abounded, flags I had previously ignored—like this dude's pride in his fifty-seven-inch TV, despite his cheapskate tendencies elsewhere. Or his three boxes of Count Chocula. Oh, and maybe that he could actually tell the difference between Count Chocula, Cocoa Krispies, and Cocoa Puffs. Or the fact that he dropped $120 on jeans for the trip to see me and made a point of telling me. Maybe that's why he couldn't afford dinner or a hotel room.

Some people need to grow up.

Look, no one wants to date a kid. Maybe you're still figuring life out. Or you don't have a job. Or you're a daddy's girl who can't let go. Or you call your parents the minute you have a question or can't figure something out. Or you're foolish and immature; you tell dumb jokes, make fun of others, and waste time on frivolous pursuits. If this is you, it's time to put your big boy (or girl) pants on. And don't think you're fooling anyone. In an age of social media frenzy, all anyone has to do is check your Facebook, Twitter, or Instagram feed to see what you're up to. Is it mostly dumb stuff? Are you retweeting Jimmy Fallon's jokes or stupid pet videos? Is your entire life told in Bitstrips? Then it's time to get a different script.

It used to be that you finished school, got a job, and got married. Now young adults are prolonging adolescence (another cultural fabrication that's pretty recent) well into their twenties. They're using the time to go to school, go to more school, travel, work part-time jobs, fret about their lack of an awesome (read: easy and high-paying) job, find themselves, move out of and then back into their parents' houses, rack up debt, and be generally directionless and despondent.

I was there. I spent a chunk of my twenties floating between a few stellar opportunities—freelance work and solid entry-level jobs—and the tricky and sometimes discouraging world of temporary employment. While a temp, I did everything from office work to counting lasagna noodles to handing out pizza samples, all the while pining after my dream job and lamenting my liberal arts education. I lived with my parents and sulked.

When you're sulking, it's hard to get your eyes off yourself. It's hard to see the future and all its possibilities. Some days it's even hard to get out of bed. But it must be done. It's part of growing up.

So if your friends are dragging you down, maybe it's time to get new friends. If you're still in school, it's time to pick a major and see it through. If you're looking at careers, it's time to get some solid internships, show up on time (actually, show up before everyone else), and be a self-starter. Ask questions. Seize opportunities. Take an interest in the real world, and get unstuck. You'll be glad you did. You'll set yourself apart from many of your peers. And you may actually get a date.

Oh, and lest you think people who are responsible and mature are also boring, let me tell you this: I never met a take-charge, mature, and compassionate single dude who didn't make me look twice at him. Maybe it's time we took this whole idea of "hotness" back and made it about more than a shallow and oversexed standard of attraction. Because you know what? Maturity is hot. Forget what all the rappers, teen idols, and baby daddies say. Some things never go out of style.

Having and keeping a job? Hot.

Respecting women? Hot.

Fighting for those who can't fight for themselves? Superhot.

Knowing and living out the Gospel? Megahot.

And, ladies, we have unique gifts too. Most of us are natural connectors and nurturers. We're good at listening, relating, and empathizing. So maybe it's time for us to stop caring more about the contestants on *The Bachelor* than we do about the people around us. It's time to stop gossiping and speaking nonsense and use our words to build others up.

Encouraging a friend? Hot.

Loving the elderly? Hot.

Being creative and serving joyfully? Way hot.

Speaking truth and knowing when to keep our mouths shut? Uberhot.

Friends, let's grow up.

## REASON NUMBER THREE: YOU'RE NOT DATING

I was in Walmart looking for a birthday card. After a few minutes of scouring the racks for a funny-but-not-raunchy one (and avoiding the musical ones; those drive me nuts), a guy about my age appeared in my peripheral vision.

"Excuse me, I'm looking for a card for my mom and wondered if you'd help me pick one out. I'm not totally sure what she'd like, and I want to find something special."

Awww.

That was pretty much my reaction. This sweet guy was doing his best to find a card for his mom! What a wonderful son! Of course

I would help him find a card! Did he want me to help him find a gift—or a special song or flowers or a timeshare in Florida—for her too? Because I would.

No, he just wanted a card.

Okay, easy enough. We read card after card until we found what he thought was the perfect one. I smiled and turned to leave.

"Hey, how about getting dinner?"

Oh. Snap.

Ladies, that is what you call smooth. Now, I don't know if the whole thing was contrived from the get-go, but it doesn't matter. What matters is that this guy had game. He got me hooked with the mom-card story, and after a suitable (though short) amount of time, he made his move. It was made so effortlessly, so naturally, I didn't see it coming.

On the other hand, I know guys who have pined after girls for years without ever asking them out.

Why the difference? Some of it is the ratio of risk to payoff. Walmart guy may have been truly interested in me, or he could've just been after a booty call. I'll never know (I panicked and turned him down). But the "ask" was spontaneous and cavalier. He didn't know me, so he really had nothing to lose. The pining guys, on the other hand, have built futures in their minds with their girls of choice. They've put everything into their dreams until the dreams are too big to risk. So they hang back, cling to the dreams, and do nothing.

There has to be a balance. On one hand, you don't want to adopt a player mentality, treating girls like conquests and asking out every one that crosses your path. But you don't need FBI files on the girls that interest you, either. You can observe, analyze, even hang around and be friends with a girl you like for only so long. Eventually you have to ask her out, or you'll get nowhere.

As I travel around and ask young adults to define *dating*, fewer and fewer can do it. It's almost foreign to them. What they are familiar with—and are settling for—is hanging out and hooking up.

Both hanging out (spending undetermined amounts of time with undefined groups of people of varying size) and hooking up (having "no strings attached" sex with a partner you may or may not know) are cheap forms of relationship that many young adults try to pass for dating. But they're not. They're both really just forms of using people, whether for pleasure or companionship.

Hooking up is never okay. Just look at STD rates, abortion rates, and emotional and attachment disorders to see that. Oh, and don't forget the Bible's perfect script for sex and relationship. Hanging out is appropriate for certain levels and stages of friendship. But it's not dating. It's not going to get you into a committed relationship that goes the distance.

In Christian circles, we tend to err on the side of not dating. Guys don't ask girls out for a number of reasons. Some are still being boys. They're caught up with their toys, their friends (buds, bros, homies), and their hobbies. They're not even in the spheres of mature, eligible women. That's probably for the best. Boys shouldn't be dating.

Others are scared. They don't want to fail. They don't want to be the guy who asks girls out but gets rejected. And rejected. And rejected.

Still others treat dating as if it were a sequel to *Mission: Impossible*. They don't want to show their hand, so they do a lot of vague reconnaissance, fact-finding, and second-guessing. They get into a girl's circle, and in an unobtrusive, completely risk-free way, they try to scope her out. But the next thing they know, she's coming to them to get advice about dating another guy—the guy who actually asked her out. Meanwhile, Mr. Stealth has been friend-zoned. And it's very difficult to get out of the Friend Zone.

Where we got the idea that we have to know everything about a person before dating him or her, I have no idea. Folks, that's the point of dating—to get to know someone! These days it seems you have to practically be betrothed to be seen doing coffee with someone of the opposite sex. Good grief, it's a huge drama fest. I've had girls from Christian colleges—attractive, smart, and friendly girls—come up to me in tears saying they've never been on a date, and they're about to graduate. Now that I think of it, I've had thirty-year-old girls say the same thing.

Guys, I believe the power to ask a girl out is in your hands. It's a great act of leadership and service at the same time. Don't worry about whether she'll misinterpret a date as a marriage proposal. If she goes home and writes her name with your last name, it's not the end of the world. If she picks out china patterns or tells her girlfriends how wonderful you are, consider it a compliment. You'll survive. You went on a date. You're a step ahead of most of your buddies.

That said, ladies, stop writing your name with guys' names. Don't pick out china patterns. Stop debriefing a coffee date as if it's Watergate or an episode of 24. Do yourself a favor and be normal, for crying out loud.

While we're at it, let's talk about why you don't date. Yes, one reason is you're not being asked out. We covered that. But some of you are unnecessarily turning guys down.

Some of you are too attached to the fifty-point list you, like me, created in junior high. If a guy doesn't measure up to the list, you turn him down. Some of you have put arbitrary requirements on men, be they vague levels of spirituality and what that should look like, the type of job they should have, or their correct use of grammar and punctuation—one transgression and he's banished from the realm of possibility. Or you've already labeled a guy as "weird" based on what you've observed or the gossip you've heard.

You also may not be dating because you're "one of the guys." It's the female version of being friend-zoned, and it's not fun. I used to be there. I was always debating guys and trying to one-up them. I used my humor to cut them down. I refused to show emotion. I acted as though I knew everything. I never asked for help. And I stood by as the guys I liked asked other girls—the warm, kind, interesting girls who weren't afraid to be girls—out on dates.

Let me summarize by saying a few things. For starters, here is something not often said that should be very freeing: guys are under no obligation to ask girls out, and girls are under no obligation to accept. Get it? There's power in both camps, and that's okay. Dating isn't a science; it's a dance. It's a mystery that involves risk, chance, and a fair share of sweaty palms.

That said, it's only dating. You're not marrying anyone—yet. If you're only going to ask out or accept the person who makes your heart instantly race, you're going to eliminate a big pool of potential candidates.

I'm a big fan of giving chances. No, I'm not saying give everyone a chance. If the person terrifies you, don't go out with him (or her). But if it's someone with a good reputation who loves Jesus, is of good character, and is in your acquaintance, you may be surprised what you learn. Don't rely on fireworks, a feeling, or the need to know everything about the person beforehand. Don't get paralyzed by all the potential what-ifs of a relationship. Because guess what—you're not in a relationship.

My mom has been in an assisted living facility for about a year now. She's already had two or three of the elderly men there interested in her, and they haven't been afraid to show it. I was lamenting to her that her dating potential is better than mine, and she replied, "Oh, I'm not going to date any of them. I don't want things to get messy."

Get messy. Start dating.

## REASON NUMBER FOUR: YOUR DATING IS DIRECTIONLESS

So you're in a relationship. Or at least you're pretty sure you are. He calls you his girlfriend, or at the very least you go out one-on-one pretty often and he (usually) pays. And you hold hands.

For now, let's call that dating.

So what's your plan? Where do things stand?

*Um, what?*

Yeah, you heard what I said. Where is this thing *going*?

Therein lies the problem.

There are a lot of you who by definition are dating, but rather than being a means to an end, your dating life is more of a holding pattern—something you define yourself with now but can't explain in future terms.

You're stuck and you don't know it.

Not that dating isn't great in itself; it is. It's a lot of fun and can be downright exhilarating with the right person. But having fun isn't the final goal. Neither is creating history and memories, keeping one another accountable, maturing one or both parties, or practicing communication and commitment.

The purpose of dating is to find a suitable marriage partner. Period. You'll have fun in the process, and yes, you'll grow (and hopefully your boyfriend or girlfriend will too), but in dating there is something to accomplish. And it's not to be treated flippantly or casually.

Again, we see extremes in this area. On one hand, the dating couple is approaching their relationship with primarily fun in mind. It's a wait-and-see attitude that elevates the thrill of dating, of belonging to someone, and of always having someone to bring to a friend's wedding or the company Christmas party. This dating is recreational. It's pizza nights, Saturday hikes, designated ringtones and text chimes, and even the occasional vacation or missions trip. It's birthday parties, endless text trails, and nauseatingly cute pet names like Boo and Baby.

But nothing's defined. There's no game plan, only the promise of hanging in there while things stay fun and carefree. You're checking each other out, letting the chips fall where they may. Eventually, one person gets frustrated with the inertia and tries to change the plan. This may or may not work. Worse, neither person addresses the inertia and the relationship dies, usually after a significant amount of time.

Remember the Count Chocula guy? The one who played it safe and paid for next to nothing? His previous relationship—the one he was in prior to meeting me—lasted nine years.

*Nine years.*

As he described it, the relationship had intense seasons, and he and his girlfriend knew pretty much everything about one another (well, duh), but in the end, without direction or purpose, it fizzled out. He told me that after nine years, he and his girlfriend met in a coffee shop, sat across a table from one another, said "It's over," and parted ways.

How incredibly sad. And how disappointing to look back and realize that there's a decade of their lives (and marriageable years) they'll never get back. But it happens all too often. Has it happened to you?

On the other hand, you have the couple who's doing more than recreational dating. They're into each other and really want to see something work out. They hope (maybe without saying anything; they don't want to jinx it) that this will end in marriage. So they'll do everything they can to test the waters.

They study each other and share intimate details from their pasts, as well as their likes, dislikes, hopes, and dreams. They spend every minute together. They fight and make up, then fight again. They're accountability partners. They're practically members of each other's families, even celebrating holidays in each other's homes. In short, they're pretty much married—they certainly act like it. Their lives are totally enmeshed. But they have nothing to show for it. It's not real. They're playing house.

Both cases above become even more serious when you factor in the physical. How hard is it to be into someone and dating him or her exclusively, with little to no structure, yet hold to a biblical view of sex and purity? I'll answer for you; it's pretty difficult.

This is why we see people dating for three, four, or five years (or nine), and we're not surprised to learn that they're sleeping together and/or living together. It's inevitable, isn't it?

We think we're going to navigate a relationship with virtually no plan, no boundaries, no accountability, and no objectivity and escape unscathed? Hardly.

But don't you need to know what you're getting into? Don't you need to learn everything you can about this person, especially if you're hitching your wagon to theirs for life?

Not really. There are some big things you need to learn, yes. We'll get into that later. But the idea that you need to practice life with this person is wrong. The idea that you need to test him or her out sexually is wrong.

Cohabitation is so bogus. Take the Bible out of the equation, and experts still agree that there are absolutely no benefits to living together before marriage. In fact, living together is actually worse for long-term marriage stability and happiness.

Couples who live together before tying the knot do not get to marriage faster. In fact, living together acts as a major de-motivator to marriage, especially for men (hello, milk/cow). Plus, those who cohabit have higher rates of divorce once (if) they do marry. They also have higher rates of domestic violence in the relationship, more disparity among who does chores and takes responsibility in the relationship, and less commitment to the relationship in general.[2]

Finally, living together keeps people in bad relationships longer. It's almost like the frog-kettle scenario: they've paddled in the same pot for so long they don't notice the steam rising out of the warming, and now boiling, water.

She may see that the relationship is not ideal. In fact, she and her boyfriend have a lot of problems that seem to be getting worse, not better. But they share rent. And they bought those rugs, dishes, and houseplants together. And now they have a dog. It's just too difficult to leave now.

And so it goes.

Friends, don't date without a plan, a purpose, and a goal. Dating for any other reason than marriage sets you up for failure. You'll compromise purity by having connection (and hormones) without commitment. You'll frustrate each other by having differing expectations at different points of the relationship. And you'll waste some (maybe many) of your marriageable years by clinging to a relationship that is exclusive but has no guarantees.

By the way, everything I've said above is also why I'm not a fan of teens dating. Who thinks a sixteen-year-old should be in an exclusive romantic relationship with no power to act on the feelings, assumptions, and connections made? It's just silly.

We'll assume that most of you reading this are out of your teens and in a position to marry (and thus in a position to be dating), but if you're dating with no direction, you're no better off than the high schooler who's preparing for prom.

## REASON NUMBER FIVE: YOU'RE STUCK IN A FRIENDLATIONSHIP

It goes something like this:

Ben and Ashley are friends. Maybe they met at school or church, in their singles group or small group, or at a party. They struck up a conversation, joined in a few group activities, had fun, and decided to stay in touch.

As friends, they hang out. They hang out a lot. Eventually Ashley starts like-liking Ben. She doesn't know how it happened, or when, but it happened. Now he's all she can think about, and she starts hoping for more.

Meanwhile, Ashley and Ben are becoming best friends. They do a lot together: dinners out, movies, game nights, long talks on the phone, texting throughout the day. They have inside jokes, non-verbal cues, and, when it matters, each other's back.

Ashley's starting to wonder when things are going to change. After all, it's pretty obvious that Ben loves being with her. He calls her at unexpected times, brightens her day with a joke—even brings her a latte (extra hot, no foam) at work when she's having a tough day. Ashley knows Ben wants to be married someday; he's said so. And she's started bringing up the subject more and more. She even made Ben look at engagement rings ("just for fun") on their last trip to the mall.

How long will it take Ben to make a move? When will he wake up and realize what he has right in front of him? Surely he's seen every romantic comedy from the 1980s where that exact thing happened?

Ashley decides to bide her time. After all, she can't give Ben up now. She loves him. And she knows he's the One. They're meant to be; he just doesn't know it yet. She turns their usual hangouts at her apartment into an opportunity to cook Ben's favorite meals and show off her decorating skills (the new throw pillows and coffee table were expensive, but men love a cozy home). He notices, and she offers to decorate his apartment, which he accepts.

One night after dinner, before Ashley pops in the Redbox DVD that Ben brought over, Ben says he needs Ashley's advice.

"Of course," she answers. "Anything."

"I'm wondering what you think of Kate. The new girl at church."

"What about her?"

"Well, I think I'm going to ask her out."

Ashley, dear readers, is in a friendlationship.

By this time, Ashley is either faking calm or bursting into tears. She's rationally beginning to assess (read: subtly or not-so-subtly tear down) Kate's merits verbally, or she's throwing Ben out of her apartment. I've seen both.

Poor Ashley. What a mess, and she didn't see it coming. Most don't. And guys, you're not immune to this. I know many men who've fallen victim to a friendlationship—being a girl's confidant, buddy, fix-it man, rescuer, comforter, chauffeur, and more—all because he hoped to win over a heart that had little chance of being won. Guys too often play the role of honorary girlfriend, letting women use them, abuse them, and toss them aside when the guy they really want comes calling.

So what about Ashley and Ben? She confronted him, of course, wondering how and when this whole Kate thing came about and how could he be interested in Kate after meeting her once—maybe twice—and for that matter (the volume escalates here), what would he call what he and Ashley were doing the past year and a half?

Friendship, of course.

"What? Ashley, we're just friends."

Just friends.

There's fault on both sides here. Ben's at fault for singling Ashley out—even in friendship—and building connection with her that he had no intention of making good on. He wasn't planning a future with her. He wasn't even evaluating her as potential spouse material. Nope, he was using her for companionship now.

But Ashley let it happen. She gave freely—too freely—of her time, attention, affection, energy, and resources to a relationship that had no definition, no understanding, and no protection for her quite-fragile heart. She settled for scraps in hopes that she would someday be invited to the table. Sadly, many do this, even giving sex as a means of securing a guy or girl. It doesn't work.

I had a friend who did this. She lived Ashley's story for seven years. At the end of the seven years, she realized two things: first, her relationship with this guy had become an idol; second, it wasn't going anywhere.

Saddened but resolute, my friend sat down with this dude and broke up from a seven-year *non-relationship*. He, of course, threw up his hands and denied the time and intimacy that had been shared.

My friend went home and sobbed for days. It was like a divorce, and rightly so. She'd given a lot—too much—and *after almost a decade of investment* had walked away empty-handed. What she lost was a span of seven years—prime dating years—gone because she was fixated on a guy who never intended to pursue her. She will never get those years back.

This doesn't have to be you. How can you safeguard against the friendlationship? Start by taking to heart all the advice I've given so far. Have a realistic yet hopeful view of marriage, an understanding of what dating is, and a game plan for getting there.

It also helps to know your worth. God created you for a reason and it was good. He doesn't intend for you to drift in and out of go-nowhere relationships. If he has marriage in your future, it will be to a guy who knows you're worth pursuing or a girl who sees your value as pursuer. If he's not scrambling to treat you with care, win your heart, and claim you for his own, he doesn't deserve your special attention. If she brushes you off, wants to just be friends, or ditches you on a whim, she doesn't deserve your unique protection and pursuit.

Evaluate the time you spend with the opposite sex, particularly those you may be attracted to. Are you hanging on with little to no encouragement? Move on, and save yourself a friendlationship or worse.

Now that we've explored a few things *not* to do, what are the habits and behaviors that you want in your life, the ones that will set you on a healthy path toward marriage? Here's some good news: there are things you can start working on now, whether you're in a relationship or not.

# CHAPTER 5
# ARE YOU MARRIAGEABLE?

After college, I spent months looking for full-time work. This was partly because I graduated with degrees in English Literature and Communication (prompting my parents to give me a T-shirt that read, *I have a liberal arts degree. Do you want fries with that?*) and partly because I had done virtually no preparation for my entry into the job market. Determined that my good grades and winsome personality would land me the perfect job, I was deflated when after four months I was answering phones for a hardware store.

After having numerous temp jobs and submitting enough résumés and cover letters to paper the Taj Mahal, I was in tears. My dad, always known for his brutal tact and real-world expectations, sat me down, looked me in the eye, and asked frankly, "Lisa, are you even employable?"

To be honest, I wasn't sure.

The same question can be asked as we anticipate marriage. It's easy to go on dates, write flirty Facebook comments, and talk *about* marriage as though we know anything about anything. *Doing* marriage is a whole different animal, and it requires preparation.

Especially in this day and age in which many have seen or experienced less-than-ideal upbringings, attitudes, and examples, it takes intentional effort to arrive at marriage with optimal spiritual, relational, and emotional health.

Now don't misunderstand what I'm saying. I'm not saying the qualification for marriage is perfection or having arrived. If that were the case, we'd all be single. Marriage is a great training ground for many things, and if you're not messed up going into marriage, you'll find things in marriage to mess you up. But I currently work for an international ministry that has spent more than thirty-five years helping people patch up their marriages and families. A noble and needed thing, for sure, but wouldn't it be awesome if we could start our marriages on a strong foundation to begin with?

Let's try.

Preparing for marriage is made up of a bunch of stuff. Some of it is stuff you need to do within yourself. Some of it is stuff you need to do for and with others. And some is stuff you need to learn about marriage and what goes into uniting yourself with someone else for the rest of your life. No small task, eh?

Ultimately, you need to determine if you're in *a position to marry*. Remember when I said you shouldn't date unless you're doing it for keeps? Until you can do it with purpose, namely, to find a potential spouse? Well, this is where the rubber hits the road. Guys, before you ask that girl out, ask yourself if you could take a successful relationship with her to the finish line. If your first date turns into a second one, and eventually into a serious relationship, are you able to move that relationship in a suitable amount of time to engagement and marriage? Do you have a job? Are you motivated? Does your life have direction? If not, you shouldn't be dating.

Asking these questions doesn't imply that you're rich or have your future mapped out. It doesn't even imply that you're debt free or in a settled career. Too many young couples put off marriage until they've checked off a bunch of "stability" boxes. This is unrealistic. Your starter home will likely not be a two-story Georgian with hardwood floors and granite countertops. It shouldn't be filled with Ethan Allen furniture purchased mostly on credit. It doesn't need cable, a big-screen TV, or ten-dollar-a-pound coffee for you to grind and brew in a top-of-the-line French press.

Believe it or not, it's okay to marry poor. People used to do it all the time. It's okay to work a couple of jobs at the start. It's okay to rent, have bad carpet, drive a junky car, and live on a limited entertainment budget.

But it's generally not okay to be directionless and disillusioned. If you can't hold a job or are too good for the jobs available to you, that's a problem. If you're a perpetual student because you can't decide on a career, you have some decisions to make. If you're living off of Mom and Dad or are wallowing in a makeshift frat house with your similarly stunted friends from high school or college, you have work to do.

Get out of bed, get a job, get a budget, get accountability, get busy. Ladies, some of the above applies to you too. If you want to someday hitch your wagon to that of a quality guy, it's time to start living like you're planning to marry.[1]

This does not mean abandoning all sense of self and the dreams you've held. It doesn't mean forgoing an education or travel or career. But it does mean setting some priorities.

It means looking long and hard at where you're investing your time and energy. I'm amazed at women who tell me their number-one goal in life is to be a wife and mother, but they're out there earning advanced degrees, working long hours in an office, or bouncing around the globe from adventure to adventure. When they finally meet guys who interest them (*if* they do—with their schedules we're basically entering miracle territory here), what do they bring to the table? Sometimes it's $100,000 in debt; sometimes it's a career they've earned and are hesitant to give up or adjust; sometimes it's a nearly impossible schedule—or even the inability to be found, for goodness' sake. ("I really like that girl I met last month at church, but I heard she's off to Nepal for a few months, then India, then Singapore.")

If you're meant to be a doctor, go for it. If you are in a ministry that is all-consuming but fulfilling, keep serving. But recognize that, while God can pluck you out of anywhere and introduce you to your future spouse, operating on the premise that you'll "tack marriage on" to whatever you're giving ultimate priority to will not generally produce the best results.

As my friend Candice Watters says, "It's the man's role to interrupt a woman's plans."[2] Does that sound hard core? It should. Marriage is disruptive; it's a game changer. In a marriage, one has to lead, the other has to follow. Look for a man whose calling you can share. Make it your calling too. There are many ways this can look (No; barefoot, pregnant, and subservient is not what I had in mind), and it's very freeing to know you and your husband are on the same team, not competing for status, salaries, and ultimate control. Are you willing to let your husband provide for your family? To exercise leadership under the headship of Christ? Maybe even to fail? This doesn't mean you never work outside the home or have opinions or exercise leadership and strength of your own. It just means that if you're going to win in marriage, two heads pulling in opposite directions will never move you toward the goal.

You also want to avoid tearing men down. I understand that men can appear clueless, shallow, inept—even unkind—but treating them like jerks won't get you far. These are your brothers in Christ, remember, and biblical standards for conduct (and for the heart) apply. No one wins when we play the comparison game or try to shame men into being better men. Men respond to challenge, but largely from other men. If you want to inspire the men around you, be inspiring, not cutting or rude. Show men that they're needed, respected, and uniquely capable of great things. I can't guarantee that it'll get you a date, but it'll sure get you noticed.

Finally, as I said to the men above, get your house in order. Live within your means. Don't expect marriage and a husband to rescue you from all your bad decisions or non-decisions. Don't call your parents frantically every time you face something tough. Own up to your mistakes. In short, grow up.

So what does a grown-up look like? What does it mean to be mature?

In kindergarten, I was in love (true love, mind you) with my brother's friend Kurt. Unfortunately, Kurt was in eighth grade and had little time or patience for kindergarteners. Knowing this, I decided to convince Kurt I was in eighth grade too. Never mind that our school was small, that I rode the school bus in the front seats reserved for the kindergarteners while he rode with the cool big kids in the back, or that I was his friend's kid sister. I was pretty sure I could pull the wool over his beautiful blue eyes.

One day, as we were waiting for the bus after school, I saw Kurt and my brother talking. Kurt was wearing a black leather jacket, which solidified in my mind the fact that he was the cutest guy I had ever seen and thus most likely my future husband.

I walked up to where they stood, sidled up to my brother, leaned against him, and pushed myself up on my tiptoes. Assured that I was now tall enough to pass for an eighth grader, I smiled sweetly at Kurt, who looked at me briefly, rolled his eyes, and kept talking. My brother, on the other hand, shook me off and exclaimed loudly, "What is your problem? Get away from me!" I didn't react as maturely as I'd hoped. In fact, I ran back to my group of friends, crying.

You see, I was a poser. No one believed I was in eighth grade, because, well, I wasn't. Not even close.

It's kind of like that when we look at adulthood. Those who are mature are easy to spot, maybe not right away, but certainly upon closer acquaintance. They've got qualities that stick. Qualities that are very attractive. And the good news is, these qualities are available to everyone. Even better, they're qualities that matter and that you can develop, regardless of your relationship status.

So whether you're dating right now or you desperately want to be dating right now, pay attention. These six things will grow you up and make you increasingly marriageable.

## 1. GET TIGHT WITH JESUS.

If you're a Christian, this should be obvious. But so many Christian young adults today have absorbed a shallow, nominal, passionless faith that this deserves special emphasis.

So what needs to happen? Well, you need to get serious about your faith. It needs to infect your life, transform your heart, and be the catalyst for every one of your decisions. Your relationship with Christ is bigger and better than any of your other relationships. He's number one.

Here's what it's not. It's not merely knowing a bunch of Bible stories. It's not having grown up in church or youth group or gone to a Christian school. It's not having Christian parents. It's not being American, retweeting John Piper or Francis Chan every few days, or going to the Passion and Catalyst conferences every year.

Living reconciled to God is your Relationship 101, and it matters. Besides, knowing who you are in Christ will help you make big decisions down the road—about marriage, for example, because you need to find someone to marry who's also tight with Jesus. Why? Because living together in marriage, in light of an eternity with God, while living out grace now is the only way to live. And it doesn't matter how great your marriage is if your spouse is going to hell, right? What a depressing thought: to be separated for all eternity from the one you love enough to give yourself to and build a life with. Don't even go there.

So put Jesus first, and keep him there. Put your future spouse firmly in second place. You'll be glad you did. And you'll have the best foundation for maturity there is.

## 2. COMMIT TO A LOCAL CHURCH.

You may think that loving Jesus is enough. It's not. Somehow this weird "Jesus and me" mentality has infected Christianity. We think it's okay to be lone rangers in our faith. In some cases, we want to listen to podcasts, watch popular preachers, pop in and out of small groups—even hike, ski, or otherwise spend time in nature—and call it church.

The Bible calls us to be part of a local church. A physical church with real people. The New Testament church kept lists of its people. It cared for its people. It broke bread together, shared things in common, and provided encouragement and correction. It also provided a space for the mandates of corporate worship and observance of the sacraments.[3]

We need the same.

Commitment to a local church provides accountability. Put simply, you need someone up in your business. This is why when I say "commit," I don't mean "sit in the back of a megachurch with your double-walled coffee mug and take in the show." I mean "get known by some people who won't forget you." If your church offers membership, join. Put yourself under the authority of godly elders, pastors, and leaders.

Listen to the Word preached. Join a Sunday school class or small group. Begin tithing. Start serving. Become a contributor, not a consumer. You'll strengthen a muscle of selflessness you never knew you had.

Get a mentor. Find an older person of the same sex, and ask him or her to lunch or coffee. Be proactive. Build a relationship that is mutually beneficial by being both encouraging and stretching. Do you want an honest assessment of who you are? Ask them for it. What are things they've observed? Is there anything immature or off-putting about your attitudes or actions? Take feedback willingly and humbly. Then act on it.

## 3. TAKE RESPONSIBILITY.

This is where you start mastering life skills and learning what it's like to be in the real world. It's everything from getting and keeping a job to managing your money, learning how to keep a household running, making responsible decisions, and taking care of the things and people entrusted to you.

It's also learning how to budget your time and talents. It's knowing when to work and when to play. It's knowing that work is good and should be done to the glory of God. It's knowing that play is also good and is to be used for refreshment and renewal, not escapism or idleness.

Train your character. You may be chafing at the bit for a promotion, but in the meantime you're stealing Post-it Notes from the office supply cabinet. Or you're fudging your time card. Or you're telling white lies to get out of commitments. Or maybe you're not committing to begin with. Each decision above is not only chipping away at your character, it's sinful—and toying with sin is a defiance of God. Reevaluate your decisions in light of how you want to honor God and others. Ask someone to keep you honest.

There's value in accepting challenges, taking risks, and doing hard things. Push yourself, and allow others to push you too. Sometimes the easy road is the right road, but sometimes it's just easy. Know the difference.

## 4. LEAD WHERE YOU ARE.

You may be young. You may be on the bottom rung at work. You may not have a job at all. It doesn't matter. You're still a leader.

You're in charge of yourself. That's a start. We just talked about taking responsibility for our own lives. That should keep you busy.

But there's more. You are needed. Everyone (certainly every Christian) is called to serve where we are and lead if given the opportunity. It may be in a role with a big title, or it may be in a small but pivotal moment where character is needed. In both circumstances, you're on display. What will you do?

I know for myself, it seems my number-one goal on most days is to make my life more comfortable. I have no problem looking out for me. But those who get beyond themselves reap big benefits. They have the chance to make a difference. They have the chance to be world changers.

Don't be afraid to be an example, regardless of your age. Remember the words of Paul to Timothy: "Let no one despise you for your youth, but set the believers an example in speech, in conduct, in love, in faith, in purity" (1 Tim. 4:12).

Finally, remember that active leadership *now* prepares you for leadership of a family in the *future*. You're in training; get as much experience under your belt as you can.

## 5. LOVE THE PEOPLE YOU'VE GOT.

I'll never forget the girl who stood in front of me, beaming, and announced that she couldn't wait to get married someday.

"That's so great!" I replied. After all, I wanted to encourage her interest in marriage.

"Yeah, I need to find a husband so I can get away from my family."
Um.

Look, I know family is hard, and you can't really trade in the family you were born into, but using marriage as an escape plan is hardly the solution. First, it's our call to live at peace with everyone.[4] Intentional strife, hatred, and discord is not allowed. Second, you'll only take your poor relationship skills into marriage. No husband is amazing enough to please you all the time. If your current family bugs you, I guarantee your future hubster will too.

And it's not just family. A great indicator of maturity is how you relate to everyone in your current sphere: family, friends, neighbors, coworkers—even your enemies.

Actively looking to bless and love those around you is a start. Are you an encourager? How are your listening skills? Are you a peacemaker in your circles, or do you spread gossip and try to one-up others when you can?

Growing healthy relationships is learning how to communicate, how to do conflict well, how to apologize and forgive, and how to own up to your mistakes. It's establishing healthy boundaries and knowing when to say no.

Above all, it's putting others above yourself as Jesus did. It's something you'll have plenty of opportunity to do in marriage; you might as well practice now.

Of course, this doesn't mean remaining in a toxic or abusive situation. Some of you may need to extricate yourselves from codependencies within your families or groups of friends. In some cases, leaving a relationship for a time (or even forever) may be the healthiest choice. Just make sure you're doing it with a desire for what's best for all parties and not out of hatred or a determination to hurt, retaliate, or make someone pay. Forgiving someone, while not necessarily forgetting or excusing behavior, is always the first step toward freedom. And it's a sure sign of relational maturity.

## 6. ACTIVELY PURSUE MARRIAGE OR THE NEXT STAGE OF LIFE.

We should always be growing and looking ahead. Where is God calling us? What's that next step in our journey to adulthood? For those of you truly called to singleness, or celibate service, it may be a new ministry opportunity or friendship. For most of you readers, it will be marriage.

How do you begin? First, you cultivate a love for marriage by understanding God's purpose for it. Then you champion God's view of marriage and your role in it.

You decide right now that marriage—and everything leading up to it—is to be approached with biblical intention. You resolve to keep God at the center of every decision you make from here on out. You allow him to shake up your plans and expectations. And you remain teachable.

In light of this, you will no doubt realize you have some things that need to change. We all do. We're all carrying baggage that was either placed on us by the generations before us or picked up of our own free will.

Now's the time to dump it.

Men, this may mean getting serious about the way you've been viewing porn. You realize it's not a solitary experience. It's affecting your relationship with God, your family, and others. And guess what. It's also affecting your future marriage. Get help.

Women, ditch the flat-out ungodly romances and crap TV or books that you've been consuming. They're porn too. They're causing you to fantasize and to go places in your mind where you shouldn't be going. Stop making excuses and choose to let it all go.

Now's also the time to identify addictions, outrageous debt and spending pitfalls, past or present abuse, bad family patterns, and anything else that's holding you back from spiritual, emotional, and relational health. Get counseling if you need it. I'm a big fan of Christian counseling that is no-nonsense, targeted, compassionate, Jesus-centered, and has a goal.

I remember going on some dates with a guy a few years back. After an evening of Frisbee golf, he turned to me and said, "This has been great, but I'll be honest with you. Dating you has made me realize I need counseling."

At first I was offended, but not for long. I let that guy go to get the help he needed. I was saved a bad relationship (or worse, a bad marriage). For all I know, that guy probably worked out his stuff and is now married and trucking along just fine. I'm glad I could be a part of that, even though it earned me a weird breakup.

The point is, God won't keep us where we are. And we should be ecstatic about that. So for those of you called to pursue marriage and who are in a position to do it, are you ready to get started? Because for most of us, we have to date first.

All right, here we go.

# CHAPTER 6
# PREVENT DATING DEATH

If you read the prologue to this book, you are aware of my love of amusement parks. Let me state it again. I love them. Love.

For years, I've noticed that some amusement parks, in addition to the unlimited rides you get with park admission, are offering special-ticket rides—rides that offer an "above and beyond" thrill and thus command an additional fee.

On several occasions, I've had the opportunity to experience these rides, either because I got comped a ticket or talked the price down at the sales booth (it's doable; try it sometime) or had a special rate due to being there for a company event or similar.

Anyway, one of these rides is a simulated skydive or "Skycoaster." The general idea is to harness two or three people together, hoist them up about fifteen stories on a thin wire to the top of a large arch, and then let one of the parties pull the ripcord, plummeting the riders down in a free fall until the wire takes over and guides them into a controlled "fly" for a couple minutes. It's supercool.

What's not cool is everything leading up to this point. Because while I will ride just about any ride, I still have unshakeable fears that grip me about amusement park rides. These usually hit as I'm preparing to ride the ride. I'm the one who checks for rust on the coaster car, frayed wires, chipped paint, and oil spills. I push on coaster seat restraints repeatedly, fearful that the ride's hydraulics have failed and I'm minutes away from an untimely death.

In light of all this, the fact that I ride the Skycoaster at all is a mystery, because much of its operation is susceptible to human error. Case in point: The last time my friend and I rode, we were guided over to a platform by three individuals who appeared to be in high school. An intricate harness system, one for each of us, lay on the floor, and we were instructed to step in. I immediately began asking about weight limits, chiding myself for eating an entire donut that morning instead of just half.

The harnesses were hoisted up over our shoulders, and the ride operators began pulling canvas tabs through various loops. Meanwhile, they were talking about the party they had crashed the previous night and how this evening there would be another party. I was frantically checking the quality of their work (did those tabs look a little thin—maybe even frayed?) and trying to smell their breath for alcohol or pot. Before I knew it, the last tab was pulled, the kids (yes, kids) stepped away, the platform fell beneath us, and, dangling from a single wire, our perilous journey to the top began.

When we got there, our only duty was to pull that ripcord. I gave my friend the honor, in part because my eyes were shut and

I was mildly hyperventilating. She pulled it far too soon, and we hurtled toward the ground, me screaming all the way.

The decision to start dating can feel like that. It's like dangling on a wire and pulling a ripcord. Or stepping to the edge of a plane's open door and tumbling out. It's a choice. A big choice, a scary choice, and on some level, a public choice. People are watching. They want to see what you'll do. And they want to see how things will turn out. Will you land safely or plummet to your proverbial dating death?

It's easy for others to remain smug and philosophical from the safe, cozy sidelines. You're the one taking the risk, for goodness' sake. You're afraid to find out what'll happen, but as is the case with most risks, you won't know until you try.

But once you pull that dating ripcord, if you make it out alive, the payoff is huge. And I'd argue it's huge even if you don't succeed in every one of your relationships. Because remember, if you're dating to marry, you only need one relationship to work. Only one *can* work, really. You'll learn from the others.

But first you have to strap yourself in. At this point (and if you've been reading carefully until now), you've checked your attitude, you've thought about some bad habits that need to change, and you know a lot about what *not* to do. But what *should* you do?

You need to cultivate a mind-set—the right mind-set—for dating. Before you tackle the nuts and bolts of dating (a practical playbook, woo hoo!), you must think about what you're trying to build. How is this thing going to play out? You can't control the other person, but what do you see for yourself? I'm not saying you need to get all existential and do visualizations or hypnosis, but a little preparation, and even pumping yourself up, won't hurt.

Start by embracing your role. Basically, this means, men, you need to be prepared to initiate, and, women, you should be prepared to respond. Does this mean that if girls ask guys out on dates they're doomed? No. But I'll certainly say it's not ideal. Here's why.

I know married women who like to gripe about their husbands' lack of leadership or initiative. It can be something small like his inability to pick a movie or pizza toppings, or something big like his refusal to discipline their children or go to church. When I ask these women when these patterns started, most of them can easily trace them back to their dating days. Maybe she pursued him. Or she always planned their dates. She sometimes paid for their dates or at least split the cost—after all, she didn't want to be a burden. She usually initiated spiritual discussions, helped him run his life, and ultimately determined the course, pace, and process of the relationship. I even know a few women who finally proposed to their husbands. At the very least, they left enough hints or issued enough final ultimatums to show their now-husbands who's boss.

And guess what? Those women are still the bosses. But they don't want to be. They want men—men who, regardless of their person-alities or temperaments, will stand up for them and their families, who'll provide, protect, and ultimately craft a courses for their fami-lies that are rooted in wisdom and courage. They are sick and tired of wearing the pants, making all the decisions, and bearing too much responsibility for their families.

But they asked for it. Because ladies, the patterns you establish in dating will carry over into marriage. If you want to marry a leader, date a leader. Marriage will grow a guy, but it won't change him at his core.

So, guys, step up. Get ready to boldly ask women out. It'll be scary. It may be awkward. You'll need practice and perhaps a few pointers. But you'll be doing the right thing.

When I say to be bold, I'm also saying to take the lion's share of the risk. That's your role too. You're going to state your intentions ("I'd like to date you") and provide a safe space for the girl to accept or reject you. In other words, you're going to lay your cards flatly on the table while she holds hers tight to her chest.[1] You'll let her respond, and you'll receive her response graciously. If she rejects you, you won't badger her or shame her. You'll say thank you.

Author Carolyn McCulley said something a while back that made this whole issue crystal clear to me. She said, "Men trust God by risking rejection; women trust God by waiting."[2]

The trouble is we're so quick to abdicate and change roles. Rather than boldly risking, men slink back into a pattern of passivity, safety, and general inertia. Women respond out of frustration by jumping to the task, taking over, and making demands. They disrespect and even bully these passive men. In turn, they are spurned and ridiculed even further, being labeled catty, crazy, or worse. I've known a couple of girls whose preferred way of attracting a man was to fight with and belittle him. They thought it showed spunk, a quick wit, and a commitment to rescuing the man from himself. One of these girls eventually saw the error of her ways and is now married. The other is still persecuting the men in her path and remains single.

Ladies, no one wants to date crazy. It's neither cute nor fun. Stop it. Men, passivity is the ultimate in all-around lameness. Don't be that guy.

So what does the right way actually look like? For men, it's a correct application of Proverbs 18:22, which states, "He who finds a wife finds a good thing and obtains favor from the LORD." Notice the word *finds*? That's an active verb. It implies action and intention, getting out there and searching and pursuing.

I'm always puzzled by guys who say they're waiting for God to bring their wives to them, or at the very least they're waiting for God to point them out. Um, when did that ever happen in the Bible, except maybe for Adam? In the stories I read, men are going to wells to find their wives or they're enlisting family members to assist in the search or they're letting women glean in their fields after discerning their reputation and marriageability. Some men even killed for their wives. This I do not recommend, but you get my point.

Your search needs to begin with a healthy amount of prayer to align your attitudes and expectations. Then you figure out who's in your circle. Because that's the most logical place to start. Observe the habits and character of the single women you know. Interact with them if you can, whether in class, at church functions, volunteer opportunities, or whatever. You don't need their complete history, just an idea of what they're about. Remember, you date to find out the rest. Then the simple but hard part: ask one girl out. Just do it.

I was speaking in a singles Sunday school class just last week, and the father of one class member was visiting. In response to this general subject, he piped up.

"When I was young and single, on Thursday nights I sat down with a pen and paper and made a list of all the single ladies I knew. Then I started calling down the list, asking ladies out for the weekend. If one said 'no,' I asked her if that meant 'no' for now or forever.

If she said 'forever,' I crossed her off the list. I went on quite a few dates that way."

I cracked up at this story, mentioning to the class that this approach generally only works for certain personality types (and certain girls). And maybe it had a higher success rate decades ago, back when this dad was on the dating scene. You don't want to come across as a mac daddy player. And you certainly don't want girls to be one on a vast list of possibilities; no one feels special or singled out that way. While perhaps overzealous, I like this dad's confidence and sense of purpose. Some men could learn from that.

Find, find, *find*. If you need to tack it to your mirror, do so. "He who finds a wife …" not "He who sits around assessing a woman to see if she's good enough, then does reconnaissance to determine her level of interest, then invites her on a vague non-date to 'see what happens.'" Know the difference.

Ladies, what does your search look like? It may not appear as the outright pursuit it is for the men, but trust me, it's no less active.

As I alluded to in chapter 2, the first thing you women need to do is admit you want to be married. Yeah, sounds dumb, but it's true. I remember one time in my thirties making reference to the fact that I would love to be married. "Really?" said one of the folks I was with. "I always thought of you as a career woman. I've never heard you mention marriage, and you certainly have never seemed interested in it."

Aack. That statement had more truth in it than I cared to admit. We women seem to carry around a lot of shame when it comes to our desire for marriage and family. For some reason, we feel like planning for marriage (or even hoping for marriage) means that we're desperate or not trusting God. This is so wrong. God has placed a desire for marriage and family in most of our hearts. Remember how marriage and family are God's ideas?

I don't mean you need to get all "name it and claim it" over marriage. God has a different story and timeline for each one of us, and his will rules. But if you feel called to marriage, don't be ashamed to say it. Don't be ashamed to prioritize it, prepare for it, or pray for it.

That's where you begin: prayer. Then you also begin opening your eyes to the men in your acquaintance. Get to know them. Serve alongside them. Ask others about them, especially respected married persons who may be able to vouch for them.

Treat them with kindness, not to the exclusion of others, but there's nothing wrong with showing a little special interest. Is this flirting? Maybe. But I'm not opposed to a little flirting. I am opposed to game playing, immodesty, and manipulation. Letting a guy know you're alive is a totally different story. There are good ways to get a guy's attention. I love what I read a while back on this front: "It is for men to strike out into the forest and look. It is for women to crack the twigs and stir the leaves so we know where to find them."[3]

One final word on pursuit. Why is it that we're all gung-ho about being intentional in every area of our lives, but when it comes to marriage, we throw up our hands and back away? If you're looking for a job, you don't sit in your apartment with the lights out, saying, "I wish I had a job. I hope someone knocks on my door and offers me one." No, you scour job listings, craft a résumé, network like crazy, and apply and interview until you get a job. If you need a place to live, you don't sit on a street corner and hope someone pops by with an offer you can't refuse. You look at housing classifieds, put up "apartment wanted" posts, ask your friends for leads, and so forth.

If we're this intent on finding jobs and accommodations, how much more intentional should we be in finding a mate? The answer is clear. Does this mean all the work is on us? No. God's got his hand in it too. He'll move people into your sphere, provide divine appointments, point things out to you, and prepare you along the way. But as the popular saying goes, "It's easier to steer a moving object." Get moving.

What else needs to happen in your search? Well, you need to start paring down your marriage "must-haves" list. Whether it has fifty or five hundred items on it, you need to get it down to about five. They are:

- Is a true disciple of Jesus (someone in whom you see evidence of real Gospel transformation as outlined in the Bible)
- Is actively growing in his or her faith (no long-term stagnation or stall-outs)
- Is in a position to marry (time to get that job, guys!)
- Is humble and teachable
- Is someone who has a similar calling or whose calling you can join

Obviously, psychologists and even theologians like to add things to this list. For example, a conversation on children, goals, extended family, and other important subjects needs to happen. But for now, start with the above five. You'll have plenty to work with.

That said, I don't want you to end up where I was in my late thirties. To make up for my twenties, which were in effect a dating ghost town, I swung the pendulum completely to the other side and entered the era of Too Many Chances. Beyond a guy being a Christian, I didn't have too many other criteria for dating him. I gave every guy a chance. Sure, I went out a lot and even ended up in several relationships, but they were a waste of time.

I considered beginning a relationship with a guy halfway around the world despite the fact that we had pretty significant doctrinal differences, he used way too many endearments and shared too much personal information for the level of our acquaintance, and there was a pretty big cultural chasm between us. Oh, and we had never met.

And there was the guy who didn't like much about me. He criticized my sense of humor, my personality, my family, even the way I lived out my faith. I dated him for at least four months.

And the guy who took me to coffee, and in less than ten minutes I discovered he was neither a Christian nor single. At the first mention of his wife, I had the sense to end the date. Wow, such discernment.

One way to avoid such silliness is to date in community. Get a team around you. Fill it with people who know you, love you, and will not let you get away with a bunch of crap. Tell them about every person you're meeting. Allow them to evaluate each potential date. Give them permission to ask tough questions.

And here's a scary one: pick three people—mature, godly, no-nonsense types—and give them veto power. If all three agree that the person you're dating (or about to date) is an unwise choice for very good reasons (which they are willing to share), you're done. You rely on their wisdom and objectivity, end the relationship, and move on. This will save you from a whole truckload of foolishness; trust me.

Finally, avail yourself of the books, sermons, articles, and studies on relationships that are out there. Read up. Get good counsel. Take notes, and start applying what you learn. One word of caution: don't amass so many books that you spend all your time reading and no time practicing what you're learning. Having a library of marriage books doesn't get you married.

Armed with this knowledge, community, and framework for action, you're ready to start dating.

# CHAPTER 7
# "SOOOO, HOW DO I ACTUALLY START DATING?"

I had just finished leading a dating seminar in which I thought I'd shared a wealth of wisdom. I had issued many principles like the ones I'm sharing here, so I was pretty confident my audience could take it from there.

I was wrong.

After I had finished speaking, one guy immediately shot his hand in the air.

"Yes?" I asked mildly.

"Soooo, how do I actually start dating?"

You've got to be kidding me.

In truth, I thought he *was* kidding. He wasn't. The poor guy didn't have a clue. I soon learned that he grew up without a dad, saw few examples of healthy relationships, and had yet to find a girl who truly interested him. Now at a secular university with nothing but a hookup culture as the outlet for opposite-sex (emphasis on *sex*) relationships, he was at a loss on how to start a relationship right.

Maybe you're in the same spot. You're not sure what the rules are. You're uncertain if dating is what you see on TV or what you've read in Jane Austen's novels. Which is right? Or is there a right way at all?

I'm not going to use this space to argue dating versus courtship or specify the exact things that must happen for your dating life to be successful. Sadly, there's no magic formula. If there were, I would've used it long ago. But there are definitely proven principles and standard operating procedures that will up your chances of dating in a healthy way that honors God, yourself, and others. They'll also help safeguard your sanity when the "anything goes" daters are either twiddling their thumbs, freaking out, or crashing and burning at every turn.

So let's say you found a girl that you want to ask out. What do you do? Remember, you're not going to play games, slink away, do reconnaissance, or become her buddy.

No, you're going to ask her out.

You do this by asking her on a date, indicating that you would like this date to happen at a particular time and in a certain place. You don't say, "We should hang out sometime," or "You'd be fun to do a movie with." These statements are vague, weak, and maddening for single women. Really, guys. This is the kind of obtuse tomfoolery that drives women to eat pint upon pint of Ben and Jerry's. It makes us bite our nails, email old boyfriends, and watch reruns of *Buffy the Vampire Slayer*. Help a girl out and call this thing a date. It means you're singling her out with the intent of getting to know her better. It means she interests you, possibly beyond friendship. It means you're serious.

It also helps if you give her a specific reason for singling her out. Do you have things in common? Do you admire the way she serves at church? Do you like her sense of humor? Even a "You seem like an interesting girl" is better than nothing.

Ideally, you ask her in person or on the phone. I understand that it's now widely acceptable to ask someone out by email or even text, but personally, I'm not a fan. I think that's the domain of scaredy-cats. Guys who are in it to win it ask in a direct and personal fashion. You'll have much bigger challenges in life than getting a date, so let's keep this in perspective. Remember, the worst thing she can do is say no. Actually, the worst thing she can do is laugh in your face, tell all her girlfriends, then post a play-by-play of your conversation on Facebook or Twitter, but let's try to forget the worst-case scenarios at this point.

Speaking of Facebook and Twitter, it's never okay to use one of these platforms to ask for a date. The fact that I even have to say so is concerning. Talk about careless, haphazard, and minimal effort. Gross. But there are even worse ways, believe it or not. I once had a guy ask me out via Words with Friends. He played his turn, then shot me a message within the game. It was a veiled ask/non-ask, and I called him out on it. He didn't know who he was messing with. Do it right, guys. Whatever the outcome, you can stand tall knowing you took the risk.

Ladies, this is where you come in. First, let me back up for a moment to say something that most women rarely think of: if you want to get asked out, make yourself available to be asked. I don't mean for you to simply be single or to say you want to get married, though both are a great start. What I'm suggesting is that you make it relatively easy for a guy to ask you out. If you migrate in packs around church or school with your girlfriends, that's a difficult (and scary) scene for a guy to break into. Strike out on your own once in a while. Sit alone at a party. Stay at home occasionally (not drumming your fingers near the phone à la *He's Just Not That Into You,* but going about your business like a normal person). Be somewhere where you can be found. And this should go without saying, but be kind, friendly, and approachable. Girls who are approachable have a better chance of being approached. No guy wants to take his chances with the smart-aleck girl who belittles the single guys, even in jest.

So you've done this, and now a guy's standing in front of you asking you out on a date. He's probably visibly shaking, looking kind of shifty-eyed and faint. Or he's acting over-the-top cool, trying to play this whole thing off as if he were Kanye West. Don't believe a minute of it.

He gets the words out, and now the ball's in your court. He's (hopefully) asked you a direct question. He deserves a direct answer. First, thank him for asking. Acknowledge that it's an honor he has singled you out. Affirm him for taking the risk. Then give him a yes or no. You may want to use a few more words, of course. You don't want to appear robotic. But your answer should be clear.

This is especially challenging if your answer is no. Most of us, if we have any heart at all, want to preserve a guy's feelings. We don't want to make him feel bad if we're going to turn him down. That's understandable, but it's no justification for confusing him with a bunch of gibberish that amounts to nothing more than a brush-off. My friend insists that women need this spelled out for them because we think we can be direct, but in the moment we freeze up, say yes, and find ourselves on a mercy date. Mercy dates are the worst. To that end, here's what a kind but clear rejection may sound like: "Thanks so much for taking an interest in me, Jeremy. It's really an honor, but I'm not interested in dating you. I appreciate your asking, though, and wish you all the best."

It sounds a bit abrupt, I know. But it works. And notice I didn't say, "I'm not interested in dating you *right now*." If you have no intention of ever dating this guy, don't give him false hope.

Men like to hear news (even bad news) straight. This is why saying dumb stuff like "I'm taking a break from dating," "I'm working on myself right now," "I'd like to grow our friendship first," and other flat-out lies are a disservice to the men around you (and yes, ladies, unless you're in rehab, a nunnery, or are truly unfit to date, those are lies). Be a woman of excellence. Stand up tall, smile, and in a clear voice give the guy your answer.

And here's the kicker: if this guy is someone you see often, at church or school, for example, continue to be kind to him. Don't avoid him or hold his asking you out against him. Show him he's valuable. He's still your brother in Christ and is worthy of gentleness and respect.

One other word for both men and women on the matter of friendship: I hear many singles, primarily those who are in mixed-gender groups that socialize a lot together, say they are hesitant to date folks in their sphere of acquaintance because they don't want to ruin the friendship. This is so lame. By the time you're out of college, your opposite-sex friend group should be dwindling. Because, quite frankly, you don't have time to invest in all those people. Furthermore, if you're afraid to risk dating one or more of those friends because you fear things becoming awkward if it doesn't work out, you're eliminating a highly eligible pool of dateable people.

Do you really need all those opposite-sex friends? Nope. If you're marriage-minded, what you need (and want) is a spouse. So don't make those friendships a priority. If you do, you'll be ten years down the road with an unwieldy gaggle of friends but no spouse in sight. Risk your friendships for something more. You'll be glad you did.

Okay, so you've landed a date. Congratulations! Now what? Again, a few guidelines will get you started on the right foot.

Guys, remember that you're calling this a date. Never forget that. Don't backpedal and make it a hangout. Call it what it is. Get your game on. Girls, remember, it's *just a date*. Don't marry this guy in your head. Be sane.

Whether the guy picks the girl up or meets her somewhere is negotiable. In this day and age, some women are skittish to be picked up by a guy they don't know well. It may be safer to meet him somewhere. Fine.

If you do pick her up, be on time. Open her car door and basically every door you encounter that evening. Go big on the gentlemanly behavior; it'll serve you well. Dress appropriately for the occasion. Don't try too hard if the circumstance doesn't warrant it, but don't be a slob, either. Girls, dress modestly. You shouldn't be advertising anything. Period. You can be cute without being trashy. Don't put your date in a position to stumble while at the same time compromising your reputation. As I tell the high school girls I mentor, "You're not Santa, so leave the 'Ho Ho Ho' at home." Yes, I just said that.

Guys, pay for the date. Every part of it, every time.

This is standard operating procedure. I don't care if you call me old-fashioned. It's an opportunity to lead and set a precedent. Strapped for cash? Plan a date that's inexpensive. Get creative. Terminally broke? Then you probably shouldn't be dating.

Paying for a date with no hesitancy or complaining is an easy way to up your hotness factor. When the check for dinner arrives, take it. Immediately. Don't stare at it, look at it and put it back down, or comment on how it's more than you expected. Your date will immediately feel uneasy. It's about this time in the game when I used to pick up my purse and pull out my wallet. I simply hate the ambiguity of not knowing what to expect. Sadly, I've been on a couple of dates where the guy let me get the check. Other guys offered to split it, and I could tell they thought they were doing me a favor. They were. They reminded me why I don't date guys who are cheap.

Single women already suffer from feeling unworthy of being cared for. We're used to fending for ourselves. It's a wound we carry but rarely reveal. You have a great opportunity here to fulfill a protective role of sorts. Don't let it pass by.

Want even more hotness points? If you're out with a group of girls (I won't judge here), pay for all of them. Foot the bill for their lattes, fro yos, or meals, and you will never be forgotten. In fact, you will have funded your own dateability PR campaign. Money well spent.

As for the date itself, there's really no formula. Pick something fun and low-key. It could be dinner, coffee, or something a bit more adventurous. A first date, however, isn't the time to stage something akin to *The Amazing Race.* Don't go overboard. Remember, the goal is to get to know this girl. That's hard to do when you are completely out of your element and/or fearing for your life. Do, however, have a plan. It's crazy-making for a woman to hear, "So, what do you want to do?" after a first date has been accepted. Put some time and thought into it. Assure her that you've got this.

If you've ensured that the date will allow for good conversation (which you should), prepare some good questions. This applies to both parties—men and women. If you'd like to know more about your date's job, family, hobbies, or faith, be prepared to ask about them. Be specific. "You grew up in Iowa, so what in the world made you decide to become a marine biologist?" is a lot better question than, "Tell me about your job."

Be careful, however, not to take on the role of an investigative journalist. This is a date, not an interrogation room. No one wants a date that plays out like a Barbara Walters interview. Be open, friendly, and casual with your questions. You'll have important things to find out about this person if this date turns into a second and third, but for now, have fun.

Here are a few additional things, in no particular order, to keep in mind in those first days of dating:

## DON'T MONOPOLIZE THE CONVERSATION.

This is why it's good to have questions prepared (in your head, not on paper, your phone, or a whiteboard). Believe it or not, you like to talk about yourself more than you think. Don't be a conversation hog. As I said before, you don't want to interrogate, but too much talking on your part wears your date down. Besides, it shows that you're insensitive, if not egomaniacal.

## DON'T TALK ABOUT YOUR EX.

This should go without saying, but no one wants to hear (yet) your sad tale of why your previous relationship didn't work out. No one wants to date a downer.

## PUT YOUR SMARTPHONE AWAY.

Seriously, people. Checking your phone on a date—or worse, responding to calls and texts—is the height of rudeness. You decided to go out with this person. Leave your other conversations, as well as your Twitter feed and Facebook wall, behind for the night. Silence your phone and stash it in your purse or pocket. Don't even take it out, except maybe for a first-date selfie if things go well.

## LEAVE THE ECCENTRICITIES AT HOME.

You have hobbies and habits that make you unique. I get it. But a first date isn't the time to put them on display. You're not being fake in keeping them under wraps; you're being wise. Your Star Wars action figure collection, Doctor Who obsession, knowledge of all NSYNC lyrics, or your "let me show you what a truly double-jointed person can do" demonstration can wait. Because guess what. You are way more than all those things. Prove it. My love of Bill Gaither and all things southern gospel is a documented fact. But when I bring it out on dates (and I have—lesson learned), it's not long before my date starts showing signs of flatlining. The fact is, I haven't earned the right to wax on about how the power ballad "It Is Finished" changed my life (which it did). I need to build some equity with normal-person behavior first. There will be time to reveal the true you (assuming the true you is tempered by normal things; if your hobby is all there is to you, you've got bigger issues). That time is not now.

## END THAT FIRST DATE PROPERLY.

It shouldn't end with making out, but it shouldn't be like adjourning a company meeting with investors, either. Girls, smile and thank him for the date. If you had a good time, say so. Guys, thank your date for giving you her time. Then, if you plan on pursuing something further, say so. Say, "I'll call you," or "I'd like to do this again." Then follow through in the next few days. Do not say anything that you don't plan to follow through on. That's lying. Walk her to her car (or yours, if you drove). Again with the doors—this isn't the time to get sloppy.

You both have the freedom to take it further from here or to end it. Whatever you do, do it with kindness and integrity. Don't string him along, and don't leave her hanging. Be adults and say what you feel.

Remember, this is just a date. You're not planning your entire future with this person. My brother-in-law missed this memo back in his dating days. Ever the frugal and practical engineer, he (on a first date, mind you) would ask the girl, "Am I someone you would ever consider marrying? Because if not, I really don't want to waste any more money on you."

I am serious. This story is legendary in our family. How he managed to get my sister to marry him is the subject of perhaps another book.

All that to say, don't get weird, overeager, rude (if you determine you're not interested in anything further), or desperate. This was a date. Your life will go on from this point, regardless of what happens from here on out. Be glad you had this experience. You're on your way to becoming a successful dater.

So let's say this goes beyond a first date. And a second. And a third. Let's say you're really digging this girl, and you want to pursue a relationship that actually may lead to marriage. As popular Bible teacher Beth Moore would say, "Glory!" I'm happy for you. Well, provided the girl's into you too. I'm, of course, assuming that.

If this is the case, you're in a great spot. This is when dating gets fun. You're no longer in that superawkward season of first dates where everything's up in the air and you're exhausted at the end of the night from being "on." Instead, you have the luxury of focusing on one individual and really getting to know him or her.

But this doesn't mean you get lazy. Remember the importance of dating with direction? Avoid those four-, five-, or six-year go-nowhere relationships by reviewing your game plan. Your game plan involves marriage. Eventually, at least. And sooner rather than later. You're having fun, but there has to be a goal.

So, guys, this is probably another time to define the relationship. If you're no longer dating around, she deserves to know that. This is when you tell her that you want to date exclusively and see what she says. If she's game, you establish parameters for the relationship. As I said earlier in the book, this doesn't mean you start acting married. You don't shut out everyone else in your life and gaze into each other's eyes 24–7. You don't become accountability partners or start sending birthday gifts to one another's parents. You certainly don't start having sex or living together.

Guys, if you're serious about this girl, this is a great time to start thinking ahead. Keep in mind a timeline for yourself so you don't get comfortable in the dating status quo. Remember, dating isn't the goal—marriage is. (I know; I keep saying that. But I have to make this point clear.)

At the same time, you may want to keep this timeline to yourself for now. I dated a guy who on our *second date* walked me through a PowerPoint presentation that outlined a timeline for our relationship. It included benchmarks for meeting one another's families, getting engaged, and getting married. In his mind, we'd be ready to get engaged at the three-month mark. Needless to say, I was a little freaked out. Not enough, apparently, because I continued to date him. We didn't make it to the three-month mark.

Thoughtful, Scripture-guided planning is wise. Heedless, me-centered hyper-planning is freaky and foolish. As my friend Bryan says, "It's great for men to lead in a relationship, but they have to look back and make sure someone's following them." One-sided relationships aren't relationships; they're fantasies.

That said, ladies, per Bryan's advice, you should generally let the guy lead. Pay attention to how he treats you, other women, and those in authority over him. See if he initiates conversations that matter—conversations about faith, goals, and the future. What's he into? Who are his influences? What's he reading? How is he serving in his church and beyond?

Marriage will shape a man, but you do not have the power to change him. Don't get serious about a relationship assuming that once you're married your guy will become everything you want him to be. The guy you want to marry should be that man right now, or he should at least be on his way there. By the way, I have a lot more sympathy for a twenty-year-old man who is making mistakes and learning from them than I do a guy in his late thirties who's making mistakes because he refused to learn from them back when he should've.

The fact is, biblically, the husband is the spiritual head of the home.[1] Notice the passage doesn't say he *should* be the spiritual head of the home; it says he *is*. Whoever you marry will be your head, so marry the man you want to lead you closer to Jesus Christ. Don't hope that a ring on his finger will somehow transform him into that man; it won't.

As you date, you're going to get more and more attached to this person. That's a fact, so this is a good time to chat about purity.

Remember when you were in church youth group and your youth pastor (or someone's dad—remember what I said in chapter 3?) taught on sexual purity? I do. Looking back, I appreciate the effort that was made, but at the time, it was uncomfortable. After all, I didn't know much about anything, let alone sex. But the way it generally went was that there was a healthy dose of teaching on Why You Shouldn't Do Anything Nasty Because It Will Make Jesus Sad and Perhaps Get You Pregnant, then you had to sign some sort of pledge promising to follow the rules. If you were lucky, your dad would take you on a cool trip (my friend's dad let her pick anywhere in the United States!), have a reinforcing pep talk (a small price to pay for a free vacation), then present you with a "purity ring."

I never got a trip or a ring. I don't hold it against my dad. After all, I was the last of six kids, and I'm sure he was grateful to still be alive at that point. Maybe he hoped one of my older sisters would fill me in. Either way, I learned enough about purity to know that it was important. More fortunately, I was both legalistic and unattractive enough (hello, glasses, braces, and perm from the local beauty school) to safeguard myself without really trying.

What amazes me is how the purity talks basically became nonexistent in college and beyond. I mean, in college, you're off on your own, living in dorms or sororities or apartments with a newfound freedom that's intoxicating. Fast-forward to post-college life and you're really flying solo. Now you're in an apartment or home with no one to tell you what to do. Add to that the fact that you have disposable income and confirmation from the world that you're free to do as you please, and it's a wonder any of us hold to any biblical standard.

Purity is important. But this isn't just about singles not having sex. Purity begins in your mind and heart. So if you're not having sex but looking at porn or reading *Fifty Shades of Grey*, you're sinning against God, yourself, and your future spouse. We need to take this more seriously as a church. Our hearts and even our souls are at stake.

What's more, it's important to remember that you're dating someone's future spouse. He or she may become your spouse, but you don't know that yet. In the meantime, you're responsible before God for treating that relationship with the utmost integrity and purity.

This is where it's good to remind yourself that you're dating a brother or sister in Christ. Brother or sister. Yes, you've singled out that brother or sister. Yes, you have romantic feelings toward that brother or sister. Yes, you're hopeful for many things. But until the ring's on the finger and the covenant before God has been made, you are brother and sister—nothing more.

That accountability team of three I was talking about makes a lot more sense now, doesn't it? This is partly why you need those godly people deeply involved in your relationship. You need them watching you, asking tough questions, and rebuking you when appropriate. You should have them heavily involved when you're dating. Don't march off as a lone-ranger couple. It's too dangerous. The stakes are too high.

So while you're in an exclusive dating relationship, don't waste your time getting physical. It'll cloud your judgment and veer you off course. Don't even waste your time getting too emotionally entangled. After all, there's emotional purity too. Don't let your mind go places it shouldn't. Don't share things that are inappropriately intimate. Don't give up too much of yourself too soon. It's not time for that.

Does this mean I draw a hard line that says no to hand-holding or hugs? Am I saying you have to save your first kiss for marriage? Am I mandating that engaged couples follow the same script as those on a first date? No, not really. I'm not issuing any kind of gospel here.

Should I have to? You probably have an idea of where your heart is and where struggles or temptations lie. If you're determined to cross lines, you'll make it happen. If you want to have sex with your date, you're gonna find a way to have sex. This is a heart issue, not a rules issue.

Err on the side of safety. Don't put yourself in a position to compromise. Know what it means to honor God with your heart, mind, and body. Decide ahead of time that you won't do anything that will capitalize on your weakness. And get objective people (no, not your boyfriend or girlfriend) to hold you to it.

Dating is not for meeting your physical and emotional needs. Dating is for determining the feasibility of a lifetime with another person, which is not done by ascertaining the kissing prowess of your partner. It's not even about your level of compatibility (contrary to the so-called wisdom of all the relationship quizzes and algorithms out there). When it's all said and done, it's about commitment. Are you ready to give the rest of your life to this person? More generally, are you ready to give the rest of your life to the Lord in this area? Remember, there are many people you can be compatible with and build a God-honoring life with. Is this one of those people? Are you ready to shed yourself and start sacrificing? Is your boyfriend or girlfriend in the same spot? Then you may have some decisions to make.

There are many great books out there on when to get engaged, how to get engaged, and what to know before you say "I do." I won't go into that stuff here. I've never been there, so I'll leave that up to the experts on that subject.

What I will say is that you don't need to know everything about a person before marrying him or her. You can't. So get counsel, ask tough questions, maybe do some pre-engagement counseling, and make a decision as to next steps. If it's time to get married, then do it. If not, determine if you just need more time (and that you need it for the right reasons, not because you're scared, lazy, or unrealistic) or if it's time to break up. If it's time to part ways, have the courage to do so. Knowing when to break up can be just as important as knowing when to get married.

# IT'S OVER

My sister dated a guy whom she had no business dating. They met at work. He understood very little English and spoke even less (but according to her, they spoke the "language of love"). He was Muslim, she's a Christian.

That was the beginning of their problems. There were more (no, really?) that surfaced over time.

But he was charming. Oh, was he charming. He flattered her, showered her with gifts, treated her protectively (overprotectively, really), and spoke her top three love languages: mystery, spontaneity, and recklessness.

This was a season of unceasing prayer for our dad. Because try as we might, no one could talk my sister out of this relationship. She was hooked. She went through emotional highs and lows while dating this guy. She made some bad decisions. She hid things from our family. She knew she was treading on dangerous ground with this man, but she just couldn't quit him.

He did everything he could to get my sister to marry him. She wanted to marry him. He was so much kinder and more attentive than other men she'd dated. He was exciting too.

But something kept her from saying yes.

Praise the Lord.

We know that it was prayer and God's protection that forced my sister to break up with this dude. But it wasn't pretty. My sister had to move to another city to get away from him. She concealed her location, because he tried to follow her. He called and left messages, pleading with her to return.

During this time, my sister suffered a broken heart of epic pro-portions. She basically went through relationship rehab. She spent her days crying and reading the Psalms. She contemplated going back to him. But in the end, she wanted to honor God. She got counseling and, little by little, picked up the pieces.

It was only months later that she discovered he had married someone else and had a mistress or two on the side.

Again, I'll say it: praise the Lord. My sister escaped. But not unscathed.

You may never walk through something this *Dateline*-esque. But if you're gonna date, chances are you're gonna walk through a breakup or two. Or twenty. Breaking up is never an ideal scenario, but for some relationships, it's the best one. Maybe you're in a re-lationship right now and, based on what you've read in this book, you're guessing that a breakup is in your near future. You're dating someone who doesn't share your faith or isn't passionate about it. Maybe that person hasn't grown up or isn't in a financial, emotional, or spiritual position to marry. Maybe you are moving in two entirely different directions. I'm sorry. But I'm also proud of you. Do what you need to do.

The key to breaking up well is to date well. We covered that in the pages leading up to this one. If you're looking out for the interests of the other person and you've conducted the relationship with integrity and purity, then, while sad, the process of breaking up should never be devastating or dysfunctional. Technically, you should be able to sit next to your ex at church and feel confident, secure, and generally sane regarding how you acted in the relation-ship and how you're acting now that you're no longer a couple.

Neither party should have to switch churches, friend groups, small groups, or schools.

That said, there's a natural season of grieving, especially if you dated for some time. If you crossed physical and emotional boundaries, the toll will be more severe. Be prepared.

When ending a relationship, just as in starting one, do it in person if possible. Be succinct and straightforward. You don't owe the person a play-by-play summary, but you should give a reason for the breakup. Be honest. Your boyfriend or girlfriend doesn't need silly "It's not you, it's me" garbage right now. Don't say, "I can't wait to meet the lucky guy who gets to marry you," because hello, that could've been you. Don't talk out of both sides of your mouth. Don't talk too much, period. Be kind. Wish him or her the best. Affirm that person as a brother or sister in Christ in a genuine and heartfelt way.

This is not the time to try to be friends. That may come later, but not now. If you're the one breaking it off, you've probably had a bit of time to process what you're going to do. Your now-ex hasn't had that luxury. It'll most likely come as a blow. Be patient.

When a relationship ends, one or both parties (but almost always the dumpee) needs an explanation for what has happened. There are hurt feelings and unanswered questions. Whenever I've been dumped, feelings of deep rejection and unworthiness surface.

My friend Jesse did something at the time of a breakup that I think is genius. You've heard of the need for closure. Well, Jesse ended a longer-term relationship and saw that his ex was hurt and confused, so he told her that she had two weeks of access to him. During this time, she could call, email, or text him with any questions she had about the relationship and the breakup. He was free to decline anything that he didn't feel needed to be answered, but he did his best to be patient, honest, and straightforward. She could also say what she needed to say. She was free to express her feelings on the matter. But here's the kicker: He told her that after two weeks, they'd be done. The relationship vault would be sealed, and the subject wouldn't be dredged up again. She'd have closure, and they'd both be free to move on.

This won't work in every relationship, but it's worth trying. And I think it's a good rule of thumb. Because when a breakup happens, it's easy to try to hold on, literally and figuratively. Sometimes we try to keep the breakup from happening, or we try to win the person back. Occasionally we use manipulation and even deceit to guilt or shame the person into giving us another chance.

More often than not, though, we just don't know how to let go. We replay the relationship in our head. We stalk our ex on Facebook, at church, or around town. We spy on him or her to see if they jump into another relationship. We process, reprocess, and overprocess with our friends, using the opportunity to malign our ex's character and do our part to make sure none of our friends think well of them.

Really, we just need to move on. Spend a few days crying (or bawling—your choice). Get out of town for a weekend. Eat some ice cream. Check out with some video games, a batting cage, or a punching bag. Stay off of social media and maybe even take a short hiatus from social events.

But then it's time to get back in the game. Your life isn't over. Let me say again, no one should have to change churches or even small groups over this. Think this through, get perspective, and then take a deep breath and bring some normalcy back into your schedule. Know that time really does heal all sorts of wounds, so be patient. You'll get there.

But maybe you've read all this and you're thinking, *Lisa, how will I ever know what it's like to go through a breakup if I can't get into a relationship to begin with? I can't even meet quality people! Seriously, I'm about to give up. Have all the eligible Christian singles my age fallen off the earth or something?*

Glad you asked.

# CHAPTER 8
# GET YOUR
# NUMBERS UP

We've all been there. You're at church, spin class, dinner, or perhaps a funeral—this may have happened to me—with well-meaning but tragically out-of-touch married folks, and talk turns to your stalled-out love life. You're lamenting your lack of dating prospects, and that one person—it only takes one—chooses to ask the Question.

"I'm no expert on the subject. After all, John and I met in high school and married when we were twenty. But I'm just wondering, are you sure you're really *putting yourself out there*?"

It's as though there's no other possible reason for your singleness. Your life apparently doesn't allow you to have contact with normal human beings. Instead, you run under cloak of darkness from your office to your car to your home, where you pop in a frozen pizza, watch old movies, refuse to answer your phone, and then repeat the entire scene every day of your life.

Unless you have a serious social disorder, this is a ridiculous scenario. Most of us are in the same types of circles as everyone else. We work or attend school, go to church, the gym, grocery store, library, and enough Starbucks franchises to meet everyone in the world at least once. Being "out there" most likely isn't our problem.

In fact, one of the biggest challenges for singles today isn't that we don't have enough ways to meet other singles; it's that we have too many. The world has opened up to us. With travel and technology, the entire globe is within reach. This is a potentially scary spot to be in.

A couple of centuries ago, you married the girl who lived down the dirt road from you. You'd grown up together. Her family farmed too. You were about the same age and, her freckles notwithstanding, she seemed like a nice girl. She'd probably make a good wife.

Or maybe you lived in a town or even a city. Your network was wider than that of a farmer, and you probably dined with a number of families who were in your acquaintance. Perhaps the train brought new blood into your community from time to time. You were invited to dances, parties, and other social engagements. Your only task was to pick from the selection of potential mates in your sphere. A little investigation into character, connections, and bloodline, and you were good to go.

Today's myriad of choices makes it hard for us to focus. Because we're not forced to look in one place, we end up looking everywhere. And we get distracted, frustrated, even paralyzed by the options before us.

Add to this the fact that in our Western culture there's no longer a standard maturity progression for young adults to move through.

As I've said before, it used to be that you finished high school, (maybe) went to college, landed a job, and got married. All of your peers were in the same boat and on the same timeline. And you all had the same goal.

These days, even for those finishing college, opportunities are as diverse and numerous as people themselves. Some will go to graduate school; some will look for work. Some will take time to travel or do missions work overseas. Some will stay near home and others will move far away. Some will marry right away, while for many, marriage is the furthest thing from their minds.

This changing phenomenon frustrates my sister Tina to no end. We were talking about how fractured the Christian pool of single young adults is, with everyone going his or her own way and how, as a result, it practically takes an MBA to map out strategies for finding like-minded singles in my city.

"It shouldn't have to come to this," she lamented. "Back when Mark and I were dating, it was obvious that church was the place to meet your future mate. We had a college group, and when you were done with college, the next Sunday school class was for young marrieds. There were no other options."

Today, we have singles groups for people at all stages of life, namely:

> college
> college and career
> twentysomething
> twenty- through fiftysomething
> older singles (if you wonder if this is you, it probably is)

single again

single parent

single seniors

And those are just the singles groups. This doesn't even take into account the Sunday school classes and small groups based on affinity. There are some churches out there with small-group directories that rival the phone book in size and scope. Are you a Harley rider? There's a small group for you. Into French cooking? C. S. Lewis? French cooking with C. S. Lewis? It's all available.

On the contrary, I've never seen a small group called Singles Who Don't Want to Be Single. Apparently that sounds a bit desperate and unspiritual. The fact is, many singles groups operate on this premise (or at least the individuals in them do), but no one wants to admit it. Instead, the group's true intentions are cloaked with bowling parties, service projects, and book studies. All of these are great things, but again, they make finding a potential mate harder than it should be.

Instead, we see the singles in these groups looking for marriage elsewhere when suitable matches are most likely under their noses. For example, many singles are looking for love online. There's no one in the church who interests them (or appears available), but somehow that guy out in Boca Raton, Florida, could potentially be the One. At least according to his online profile anyway.

Everyone's online talking to singles from other churches in other states. It's as if we're trading singles groups with one another, making a virtual experience out of what should be happening naturally in our own spheres. I'm not against meeting someone online, as you'll see later on; I'm just saying that going online to avoid the choices in your neighborhood is not the wisest decision.

Now, if there's no one in your neighborhood, that's another thing. But numbers-wise, that applies to very few of us. Maybe a small town somewhere in Iowa; I don't know. What I do know is that most of us whine, fret, fume, and give up way too early.

I remember getting an email at work from a guy who was frustrated with the lack of quality single women in his sphere.

"Where do you live?" I replied.

"Los Angeles."

Los Angeles. I've been to Los Angeles many times. I've visited churches in Los Angeles. Shoot, I know amazing Christian single girls in Los Angeles. This guy was saying he needed to try something else, because finding a suitable girl to date was not happening in Los Angeles?

Dude.

Which reminds me. A word to college students—something I wish I had known when I was in school: if you want to be married someday, take advantage of your college experience. The fact is, you will never be around more healthy, like-minded, easily accessible, headed-in-the-same-direction, single young adults as you are now. Especially if you're at a Christian college or at a church with a thriving college group. Once you leave that demographic, the pool fractures and thins, and by the time you're thirty, finding a critical mass of people in your life stage can be like finding the Holy Grail.

For the rest of us, we may need to get creative. Because let's face it. If you're out of college, your pool has narrowed. If you're out of your twenties, it's narrowed even further, and so on. But don't get depressed. There are statistics to deal with, but you don't need to be a statistic. You need to be smart while simultaneously trusting God. Remember, God's still in the business of making good matches, and if he thinks that your being married is in your best interest, he'll help you get it done.

Of course, it only takes one, right? You don't need a million great guys or girls in your life, you just need to find one to marry and build a life with. This is true. But again, with a mobile and fragmented world as the norm, there are strategic ways to get serious, and getting serious maybe involves getting your numbers up.

This is another instance when having your team in place makes a lot of sense. Because not only is the team there to hold you accountable, your team exists to help you find people to date in the first place. If you're Indian or Jewish, you're ahead of the game on this one. Both of those cultures have thriving traditions of dating with one's family and community intimately involved. It's a practice that was long abandoned by the rest of us, which is too bad.

My own Scandinavian heritage seems to scream the opposite, priding itself in a "pull yourself up by your bootstraps" mentality in which you fend for yourself at all costs. If you're a Norwegian or Swede, you can maybe ask for help if you are in a catastrophic accident and your head is severed from your body—but only because without a head, you can't really call 911. That, and no one wants the messiness of a severed head rolling around on their IKEA furniture.

I kid, of course, but the point is, your family and friends know and love you best, so shouldn't they be the most qualified to assist in such an important search? You have to be a bit picky, of course. Home in on the family members who have wisdom, practicality, and preferably a good track record in their own marriages.

Avoid the "let's get you married at all costs" types. My mom, bless her heart, has somewhat unwittingly fallen into this camp in recent years. One day she called me up to inform me of a new single guy in her church whom she felt I should meet the next time I came to visit. I asked her what she had learned about him thus far, such as what work he did, what had brought him to the area, what his family and background was.

"Oh, I haven't met him yet. I only saw the back of his head in the church service last week."

Needless to say, while my mom has prayed for my future husband most of my life and will continue to do so, she had to be fired from the "boots on the ground" squad on my marriage team. I need folks with a little more discretion on that front, thank you.

That said, put your team to work. I love the idea that my co-worker Martha and her friends came up with. They actually created marriage prayer cards showcasing their photos and names. They sent them out to their friends and family members, asking to be prayed for—specifically for marriage—as they came to mind. Brilliant.

Which brings me to my next suggestion: be willing to be set up.

Whenever I hear a single person say he or she doesn't want to be set up, I want to slap something. Usually I want to slap that person. Because this is the dumbest thing ever. It's prideful, impractical, and downright silly. You have people who actually think you're worth dating and want to take their time and risk their reputation to connect you with someone they trust, and you're going to turn them down?

Oh no, you're not.

You're going to tell everyone you know that you're willing to be set up. Again, discernment is key. You're not looking for the "You're male; she's female. I think you'd be great for each other" setups. You're looking for the setups that are done by people who've observed something in you that may be a great fit with someone they know. That's not called desperation; that's called widening your circle of acquaintance. Be open to it.

Next, make sure you're plugged into a local church. As I said in chapter 5, if you're not committed to a local church, you shouldn't be dating. You should be finding a church. Assuming you've got a church, are you serving there? Are you meeting and investing in people? Have you found the other singles in your church, whether through a Sunday school class, small group, or social network?

If you're in a small church with few or no singles besides yourself, consider looking at other churches in your community for peer fellowship. I've spoken with a number of small-church pastors about this, and every one of them told me they'd understand if the single members of their churches tried other Bible studies or social groups around the city from time to time. You don't have to leave your small church (and you should still be worshipping, serving, and staying accountable there), but don't be afraid to take advantage of the wide range of networking and fellowship opportunities that larger churches, citywide singles groups, and other avenues can provide.

Again, I can hear you thinking, *Doesn't that seem a little desperate? Shouldn't I be trusting God to bring someone to me right where I am?*

Remember my job and apartment examples? You can absolutely trust God—and you should. But there's also something to be said for doing your part. You've heard the saying that unless you plan on marrying the UPS guy, you're going to have to get out of your house once in a while. This is true. Because, although God can get anyone married using any method he chooses, if you're still single, you may want to work with some other options too.

Maybe you need some ideas. Fine. Here are a few great ways to find people and widen your circle of people in general, and singles in particular:

## SERVE OUTSIDE YOUR USUAL SPHERE.

If you're a single woman and have been volunteering in the nursery at church for five years, you've probably met a bunch of new people. The problem is, they're all moms whose main focus right now is nursing bras, sippy cups, and finding a clean shirt on any given day of the week.

Take a season and try something new. Volunteer for a committee at church. For some reason, the finance, building, and missions committees attract a lot of dudes. Or sign up to help with that Saturday workday at church, or join the group of guys who volunteer to do yard work and fix-it projects for widows.

If you're a guy, well, that nursery slot is now open. It's pretty easy to hold a baby (or start with toddlers if babies freak you out). Don't worry about diapers; the nursery ladies will be so impressed you volunteered that they'll probably do the dirty work for you.

Other options for guys include serving at church dinners, being a greeter or usher (easy way to scope out the single ladies and make small talk: "Hello, would you like a bulletin?"), teaching Sunday school, helping with Vacation Bible School, or singing in the choir or on the worship team (skip the skinny jeans, scarves, and ballet flats).

## GO ON A MISSIONS TRIP.

Churches do these all the time, but we're generally so selfish with our vacation time that we overlook these opportunities routinely. Bad move.

Not that you should be doing missions solely for the purpose of finding a mate, but if you love Jesus and people, then getting out of your comfort zone with a group of people also out of their comfort zones can be a good thing. It also provides an opportunity for you to get to know people in a short amount of time while observing them in a context of service.

My cousin decided to help with hurricane relief efforts. So did her husband-that-she-hadn't-met-yet. The two hit it off and started a courtship soon after the trip. Their story includes not only marriage, but a shared experience that stretched, challenged, and changed them both. Not a bad way to start a life together.

Another bonus of missions trips, whether with a church or para-church organization: Many of the people who do these are empty nesters. Empty nesters often have single sons and daughters. Again, we're broadening our circles.

If you can't afford the time or money to go out of the country (or city), then consider doing something closer to home. Sign up for regular work with Habitat for Humanity, a local soup kitchen, Big Brothers Big Sisters, or similar. Remember, people know people who know people who know people. Besides, volunteering for an awesome cause or organization is a lot better than sitting home and moping about being single.

## TAKE A CLASS.

Face it, you don't know everything. And if you're stuck in a rut and headed toward winning the Most Boring Person in the World award, then maybe it's time to learn something new.

It could be a skill, a language, a hobby, anything really. And one great benefit about taking a class is that other people who want to be well rounded and interesting are taking these classes too.

Here's another chance to get out of your comfort zone. Ladies, pop over to The Home Depot and see what classes it's offering. Guys, consider taking a cooking or art class. There's no need to force anything, and don't be weird about it. But if there's something you've always wanted to try, classes are great ways to do it while meeting new people in the process.

## GET SOCIAL.

A friend of mine was in a long-term relationship that recently ended. She realized that while she was in the relationship, she'd let other relationships fall by the wayside (a terribly unhealthy and dangerous thing to do). She had become completely consumed by this guy to the exclusion of every other person in her life. Now suddenly single, she had a shortage of friends and was left wondering how she could possibly start over.

It was time for her to get a life again.

An introvert, the thought of going out and meeting new people was excruciating to her. She feared new situations, unfamiliar people, and the dreaded necessity of small talk. But she did it. She had to, or risk not learning from her mistakes in order to make new friends, invest in them, and enjoy the privilege of starting over with a healthier framework and perspective. She also risked becoming a reclusive conspiracy theorist who tracks UFOs and ends up on the cover of *National Enquirer*, but thankfully it never came to that.

You may not be afraid of people, and you may have great friends. Cool. I'd still recommend you give some new people a chance. I'm not saying you need to become besties with anyone and everyone; I'm just saying it may help to share your amazing self with a few new people from time to time.

One great way to do this is to host or attend mixers and parties. You don't need to be an HGTV star to pull off a fun event. Keep it low-key by ordering pizza, organizing a potluck, or doing dessert only. Focus on the people. Invite a few folks, and ask them to invite a few people they know too. If hosting is too much for you, go to someone else's party. Go to a party put on by a church. Go alone to all the awkward parties that most singles can't stand—you know the ones: weddings and receptions, New Year's Eve parties, Valentine's Day parties. Everyone will wonder who the super-confident and mysterious person is who had the guts to come without an entourage.

If you can't stand the thought of standing in a hot room with a handful of Chex Mix, talking about work, travel, and reality TV with strangers, look into your city's meet-ups. Meet-ups are planned activities based on interest, age, and geographic location. Meet-ups exist for pretty much anything imaginable. There are book clubs, hiking groups, cycling groups, painting parties, gun clubs—the list is endless. This type of thing is great for those who despise chitchat, because you're doing an activity with a (usually) smallish group, and it's something you enjoy and/or are proficient in. For Christians, you can find these types of groups for those who share your faith. Just search online or find out through word of mouth what's going on in your city.

These are just a few avenues to get you started. And let me be clear: I'm not saying there's a magic formula for success. I'm not saying, "Do these ten steps and you'll be guaranteed a girlfriend or boyfriend." And I'm certainly not trying to rub salt in any wounds. Some of you have done it all. I get that. Most days I feel that I have too. For crying out loud, I host an international show for singles, and yet I remain single. Surely I should've met someone by now—proof that "putting yourself out there" is only part of the equation.

But don't despair. All I'm asking you to do is shake things up a bit. It was a couple of years ago that I realized I was living a pretty small life when it came to the people I knew. I sat in the same office each day and from there went to the same church on Sundays, the same Bible study (women only, much to my mother's chagrin) on Thursdays, hung out with the same friends each weekend, and so on. These are good things, but I realized that from time to time it's healthy to push myself off my sofa and do something different. It's wise to accept that party invitation even though I'm exhausted. It's beneficial to sign up for that missions trip to Mexico. Through all these things, I am challenged, grown, and blessed by the influence of the people I meet. And who knows? God may use one of these out-of-the-box experiences to introduce me to my future mate.

And now, a word about online dating.

# THE GREAT ONLINE DATING EXPERIMENT

The nice thing about having a bunch of good friends is that when one of you has a crazy idea, the others are usually willing to go along with it, either out of mutual enthusiasm or reluctant solidarity. When my friends and I decided to enter the world of online dating, we were all somewhere between the two camps.

I don't even know who came up with the idea first, but somehow, within a few weeks' time, about five of us decided we would take matters into our own hands and find love online. After all, the ads promised almost sure success, and what did we have to lose?

After first deciding which sites we would use, we began creating our online profiles. Notice I said *sites*, plural, because everyone knows that serious online daters diversify. For those of you unfamiliar with online dating, know that creating an online dating profile is akin to taking the GRE or going to law school. The questionnaires are extensive and mined from the collective brainpower of millions of (okay, at least three) psychologists and relationship experts. If there's one thing I discovered, it's that filling out an online dating profile is at times enough to make you want to stay single or at least enough to make you realize why you are.

One site promised to match me with guys based on our compatibility. As I clicked through my various answers, I anticipated chatting with charming and intelligent young men who shared my love of hiking, meatloaf, and hip-hop.

Another site allowed me to search for profiles myself based on everything from age and height to salary, education, and political and doctrinal leanings. Still another relied almost entirely on self-generated questions and instant messenger potential. This was the perfect site to troll on lonely evenings, as no sooner would I log on and GodlyMan4U would pop up on my screen with a "Hey." I'd respond with a "Hey," and he'd counter with, "How r u?" You can see the potential here.

No online profile setup is complete without a photo shoot. A sure predictor of online dating death is posting a profile without photos. After all, your photos are what get you noticed. My friends and I decided, since the upcoming weekend was that of our fall women's retreat at church, that we'd gather after the retreat and take advantage of the mountain scenery and autumn foliage as the backdrop for our sure-to-be-impressive portfolios.

For my photos, I tried to look smart but fun, modest but not frumpy, and as young as I possibly could at thirty-five and terminally single. For one of my outfits (yes, there were wardrobe changes), I wore a shirt that said, "YOU SUCK. Which is why you need Jesus." I thought it was quirky and fun. My mom said it was inappropriate and offensive.

The photos went up, and there's no easy way to describe what followed. Each of us girls got matched with various guys. Sometimes it was the same guy (awkward), and sometimes it was a guy we actually knew (more awkward).

Thus began my second full-time job for about a year. I'm not kidding. I officially gave up TV (not a bad thing) in order to keep up with my online dating life. Between reading profiles, answering multiple-choice questions, typing out open-ended questions, instant messaging, closing out profiles, updating photos, and deciding whether to acknowledge winks, nudges, virtual gifts, and other forms of cyber-nonsense, I could hardly keep up.

And, of course, this was all in addition to following my friends' progress. We scheduled frequent debriefs. Most of our tales would not be believable were they not actually true.

Here is a sampling of some of my most memorable online encounters:

## EXHIBIT A:

The guy who wrote me a note and included forty-seven Scripture references, telling me to look them up and summarize my thoughts about them. Oh, and I was supposed to use only the King James Version, because it's "the only legitimate version." Incidentally, one of the guy's photos was of him standing in front of a window. His shirt and his curtains were made from the same fabric.

## EXHIBIT B:

The (supposed) millionaire who lied about his age (forty-seven) because he wanted to marry someone significantly younger now that it was "finally time to get married and start a family." He also told me one of his favorite pastimes was giving women bubble baths. He wanted a relationship "built on trust." Maybe he meant after he was done lying?

## EXHIBIT C:

The guy who contacted me for the first time with a simple message: "I think I love you and am wondering if you will marry me?"

To be fair, I know men have a lot of interesting (read: ridiculous) experiences online too. I used to help my male friends wade through their online prospects and weed out the fake or downright crazy girls.

So why all the madness?

I think the way many go about online dating is all wrong. In my opinion, there's nothing wrong with using an online service; it's a tool that we now have available in this technological age, and it's another great way to get your numbers up when it comes to meeting new people. The problem comes when we stop using online sites as a tool and begin using them as a crutch.

That's what you're up against when you go online. You can make the dating databases search the world over on your behalf. They can find single people in Boston, Bolivia, or Bangladesh. You can narrow your search on any number of preferences, and each potential match becomes negotiable.

The problem is, this breeds a consumerism that is completely unhealthy, not to mention ungodly. With unlimited profiles before you, it's easy to sift through them like paint samples, and the people behind the profiles get lost. They're dehumanized, in a way. Meanwhile, the potential choices become almost paralyzing, because why settle on a decent prospect now when someone better may come along tomorrow?

Many of the guys I met online had been online for a long time. With anywhere from ten to twenty-five new girls being dumped into their inboxes each day, they had the luxury of being choosy. But being choosy gets you nowhere if you never actually choose. As a result, they were wasting months, even years, in dead-end pen-pal relationships with girls they never met. They would cycle in and out of correspondence, and when interest (or conversation topics) waned, it was on to the next one for basically the same song and dance.

Again, there's nothing inherently wrong with online dating. But you have to use it, not abuse it. Here's how:

Like regular dating, all online dating needs to be done in community. If you're the only one who knows you're online, that's a problem. If you go home each night and sit in front of a screen chatting endlessly with online matches, that's a problem. If you're building connection with a person and have no accountability, that's a problem.

You get the picture. This was one of my big failings when I was online. Even though my girlfriends knew I was doing online dating, none of them monitored the amount of time spent online or the way I was spending it. Before long, I found myself juggling conversations with multiple guys. I wasn't limiting my time online, and other things—my friendships, church activities, even time with God—suffered.

I got sucked into theological debates with some guys ("Christian" guys who denied the infallibility of Scripture or defended premarital sex). Truth be told, I witnessed to more guys online during my seasons of online dating than I have over the course of my life. (I'm really hoping God gives me credit for this in heaven, because I was spending about forty dollars per month to do so.) With other guys, I fell prey to the power of the pen (or keystroke, in this case). I got into deep conversations both in email and eventually on the phone. I started developing connections with these men, telling details of my life and heart that were way beyond the level of our relationship and commitment.

I wasn't the only one. One of my girlfriends spent eight hours on the phone with a guy only the second night into their online relationship. After a week, she was saying she loved him. Another girlfriend was, within days, exclaiming over everything she and a certain guy had in common while ignoring the fact that his marriage had very recently ended. These are red flags that can't be ignored, but they're easy to overlook when you're flying high on the possibilities of a new relationship.

I'd recommend doing online dating the way my friend Travis did. In short, he had a plan. He determined ahead of time that online dating wasn't going to consume his life. He shored up his real-life relationships and made sure he had a game plan for keeping the commitments and friendships he already had. Second, he picked a predetermined amount of time to give this a shot. Rather than saying, "I'll stay online until I find someone," he planned to give online dating three months and resolved to maximize those three months. Third, he narrowed the field. He wanted to limit his options to girls he could easily meet in person. This forced him to draw a small radius around where he lived. It allowed him to incorporate a couple of good-sized cities in his search, and he was satisfied with that.

With these parameters in place, Travis went to work. He took his experience seriously and began carefully reading profiles, eliminating possibilities, and making contact. He communicated online and then on the phone, and he moved through these stages rapidly. Then he asked the girls to go on a date with him, generally within a couple of weeks of initiating contact. Travis was, for a short season, going on dates almost every weekend. But lest you think Travis a serial dater or creepy predator, he was intentional about setting expectations from the start. "It was just a date," he told me. "If I didn't sense anything there, I communicated that up front, and we could both move on with minimal drama."

What I love about Travis's experience is that it shows how great online dating can be if used correctly. Relationships only become real when they move into real time and real space. Meeting someone online is a great start, but it's only an introduction. Where it goes from there determines its potential.

Finally, Travis involved others in his online experience. He let them know his timeline and asked them to hold him to it. He shared the details of the dates with trusted mentors and friends. He allowed them to ask questions and voice concerns.

Within a couple of months, Travis met online the woman who would become his wife.

So maybe you want to give online dating a chance. You want to get noticed but only by qualified and quality individuals. Well, there's a way to do that. Before you sign up for three months on six different sites, keep the following tips in mind. Properly applied and used hand in hand with the principles I stated above, they should, for the most part, keep you out of the online dating black holes. It's not by any means an exhaustive list, but it will certainly get you started.

## GETTING THE MOST OUT OF ONLINE DATING (WITHOUT BECOMING A JERK OR DISSOLVING INTO TEARS)

1. **Take your online profile seriously.** This is your first impression. If you don't have time to fill out your profile

completely, you don't have time to date online. Answer all the questions provided. Post current and quality photos. NO mirror shots, webcam shots, selfies (don't you have friends?), high school yearbook photos, or shots of you when you were twenty pounds lighter or had more hair. Nothing immodest or suggestive. Get a friend or two to read your profile and provide feedback. Is the information accurate? Are you giving too much information? Have them check spelling and grammar while they're at it.

One thing you should be thorough about is anything related to faith. Spell it out. Outline your faith and even specific doctrines that are important to you. Share a shortened version of your testimony. Put your relationship with God out front, and stick to your guns when it comes to your convictions. Don't waste time on people who don't share your commitment to Christ. Remember why you're doing this. Then, plan to check your profile and inbox regularly. It's frustrating to reach out to someone only to discover he or she visits the site only once every couple of months.

2. **Communicate promptly and appropriately.** You don't have to reach out to everyone nor must you respond. But sending someone a message that reads, "I like your profile," is lazy, and sending one that says, "Your lips are beautiful," is inappropriate. Ask a few questions. Mention specifically what about the person's profile interests you. Don't type an essay, just be casual and inquiring. Ladies, if you want to comment on a guy's profile, fine. Again, there

are no hard-and-fast rules. Personally, I don't do anything beyond that, though. As with in-person dating, I want to err on the side of giving the guy the chance to lead. If he's interested, he'll find me and/or respond to my comment or email.

If someone sends you an email or comment that's legit, get back to him or her in a reasonable amount of time. Blowing someone off is rude and communicates that this really isn't a priority for you. And this should go without saying, but never send winks, smiles, or virtual gifts. Are you in third grade? Maybe we should all boycott online dating sites until they remove these as options. What a way to encourage passivity and goofiness. Don't even go there.

3. **Kindness and common sense apply online too.** You're talking to humans on the other side of that screen. Don't be sloppy, rude, or cavalier just because you're sitting in your pajamas with a bag of Oreos at your side and *Wheel of Fortune* on mute. Don't get preachy, argumentative, or boastful. If you have a bunch of opinions to share, start a blog or write letters to the editor. Don't burden me (or your online matches) with your fringe conspiracy theories or thoughts on preterism.

Likewise, I'm sure your past breakups were tough, but whining to guys online about why you now have a hard time trusting men is not going to help your cause. Guys, no girl wants a diatribe about how women are stupid because they won't date you or how your divorce left you penniless.

If you're working through attitudes like this, take yourself offline and deal with that stuff first.

4. **Bow out gracefully.** Whether your online relationship consisted of four emails or four months of online chatting, if you're ready to end it, do it with class and courtesy. Oh, and actually do it. Don't do what I call "the fade." This is where you disappear with no explanation or your communication becomes shorter and more sporadic until the person on the other end is left to assume that you drowned in your hot tub. Something as simple as "It was nice getting to know you, but I think I'm going to move on," is fine. If you're moving ahead with another relationship, fine. If you're getting offline, fine. If you just don't like me, fine. But let me know that I can close out your profile and focus on other people. Don't leave me hanging, especially if we've gotten to know each other a bit. I'm a big girl. I'll handle it.

   I'm assuming you can handle it too. To that point, if he hasn't contacted you in a couple of days, don't send him a message that reads, "WHY HAVEN'T YOU CONTACTED ME? DID I SAY SOMETHING TO OFFEND YOU?" Goodness. If you hadn't already, you did now. Being scary and controlling is not where it's at. Give him time. He may be busy or traveling or thinking about what you said in your last message. Or he may be going on the fade (see above). Whatever. Don't get desperate and start badgering him. Don't level accusations or clog his inbox with a deluge of hellos just to maintain contact.

Which brings me to my last tip:

5. **Take a deep breath and trust God.** God cares about relationships that start online too. He's got this. If someone seems interesting and has the big stuff in place, get to know him or her. Don't rule a guy out just because he hasn't read *Desiring God*, though he's been busy teaching Sunday school and finishing up his MBA. Give him a chance.

Don't agonize over every match, conversation, or profile element. Trust that God will point you in the right direction, give you wisdom, and put men or women in your path who may be good fits. If someone closes you out or ceases communication with you, consider it a gift. If someone wants to finally meet you in person, it's exactly that, a meeting. It's not a betrothal or wedding-planning session.

Don't worry about the one that got away. You have many potential matches. There's no formula to this, and if you're healthy and looking for someone healthy, if you ask God and your friends and mentors to have your back, if you keep your head on straight and bathe the whole process in prayer, you're gonna be just fine. Wisdom and accountability are key.

Remember those deep conversations I had with guys while I was online? Yeah, so do I. Why? Because in each case, emailing turned into instant messaging sessions that turned into long phone calls, and before I knew it, I was in a long-distance pseudorelationship. These relationships had little direction or accountability. After several months of contact, the relationships ended—one on Christmas Eve, Merry Christmas to me!—and I was heartbroken. Heartbroken. Remember, most of these were with guys I had never met. I had given these relationships too much power in my life, and when they didn't turn into something more, I felt utterly rejected. One of them took me six months—six months—to get over.

That said, while it's easier than you think to get sucked in and out of control as I did, don't completely shut out the possibility of online dating, and don't look down on those who choose to do it. Online dating is no longer for the desperate or socially inept. It's not only for singles who are older, divorced, or widowed. There's no longer a stigma (or if there is, it's fading rapidly) to finding your mate online. Many of my friends have done it. Check your motives. If you're online because no one in your church is good enough for you, it's time for a reality check. If you're online because you just want to see who's available, you need some accountability. If you're online because you've prayerfully considered the men and women around you (and are still doing so), and you realize that online dating is simply another way to meet an imperfect but humble and healthy person whom you can get to know for the potential of moving toward marriage, then go for it.

# CHAPTER 9
# IT'S OKAY TO GRIEVE

Up to this point, I've said a ton about marriage and dating. I made the case that a committed, lifelong marriage between a man and a woman is the biblical default and that it's for most people. I reminded us that God's a big fan of marriage. I argued that if marriage is in your future, the time to start thinking about it is now. I laid out a bunch of principles that can get you to marriage with maximum purpose, minimal drama, and a physical and emotional purity that will set you up for optimal relational success.

Yet I remain single.

Trust me, this is a fact of which I am deeply aware. It's a weird thing to be considered an expert on something (dating and relationships) when your own experience with the subject hasn't been ideal. To put it another way, my own advice hasn't produced the result I've hoped for all my life. I don't have my fairy-tale ending. I haven't found the man of my dreams. And even though I know fairy tales and dream men aren't easy to come by, I've always secretly (and not so secretly) hoped that my story would include both. But so far it hasn't.

This makes me sad.

I get so tired of the books, sermons, articles, and generally crackpot comments insinuating that being single is like being on *People* magazine's Most Beautiful list. That singles live dream lives—a perpetual *Sex in the City* existence of designer heels, fast cars, global travel, and cocktails at midnight in the most upscale bar in town.

Here's the deal: being single is hard.

A couple of years ago, I came home after work to see that the top portion of a slat in my front fence had been broken off. I attributed it to being on a busy street, and since it wasn't too noticeable, I shrugged it off as something to be dealt with later. The next day, the entire plank was gone. The day after that, two more planks had been broken off, and by the end of the weekend, an entire section of my fence had been removed. After making the requisite grumblings about people who have nothing better to do than vandalize fences, I came to a realization: I didn't know the first thing about fence repair.

Not only did I not know how to repair a fence myself, but I wasn't even sure who to call. Are there actual fence-repair companies? Do you go to Lowe's and ask a nice, red-vested worker to direct you to the fence aisle? Is there a show on HGTV dedicated to do-it-yourself fence competitions? Maybe I needed to call a handyman. Or are fences too big a job for handymen?

In that moment, my singleness hit me big-time. Because not only did my general fence ineptitude slap me unceremoniously in the face, I realized that, practically speaking, I was very alone.

No one in the world was responsible for that fence but me.

Oh, I know I could've called someone. Guys from church would've offered advice. Neighbors have found good fence companies in the past. My brother's a contractor, for crying out loud. He knows about fences.

My point is, no one bore that burden with me. The broken fence was mine alone. And I had to do something about it.

There are many perks to being single; I'll talk about those in the next chapter. But feeling the weight of being alone is not one of them. Yes, I understand that I have friends and family. I realize that the church is meant to step in and be my family too. But it's not the same as having a person who has covenanted before God to stick with you "till death do us part." It just isn't.

The stark reality is this: I'm no one's most important person.

Yes, my mom loves me. My sisters include me in their family gatherings. My nieces and nephews provide a substantial source of entertainment and joy. I'm welcome in our family circles during holidays. But no one is uniquely mine. My sisters and brother have their own families now. They are their priority. Apart from my mom and one sister who is still single, I have no immediate family. And they live a thousand miles away.

This is a grief that comes with singleness. Another grief comprises the losses I've experienced as a single. Because, while life goes on and God's mercies truly are new every morning, I can't deny the fact that time marches on, and with it go many things.

For example, I will never get married in my twenties or thirties. Those days are gone. This is an irreversible reality. I will never be a young mom and may never be a mom at all. The stories my friends have, those stories that include getting married straight out of college, having babies they are now homeschooling and driving to soccer practice, are stories that will never be mine.

My dad won't be at my wedding. He died when I was thirty, so the dream of having him vet potential boyfriends, give his blessing on my eventual spouse, and then walk me down the aisle is a dream that will never come to fruition. My mom is eighty-six years old. Will she be at my wedding? Will there be a wedding? Only God knows.

There are also fears that come with being single. Some of them are simple fears, like when I slept alone in my house the first night after it was broken into and vandalized. Or when I was stranded with a flat tire late at night in a deserted rest area along the interstate, racking my brain for someone to call who wouldn't be put out by an inopportune call from a single girl who didn't know what to do.

Some fears are bigger and more complex. Lately my fear has centered around growing old. My mom is now in an assisted living facility. She has daughters nearby who visit her, take her on outings and pick her up for family events, manage all of her medications, appointments, and finances, and advocate for her general care and well-being.

Who will do that for me? Even typing the question quickens a sense of fear in me. I've been to retirement homes and nursing homes and seen people who have no one—the people who sit alone day after day with no one in the world to call their own, or perhaps just no one who has made them a priority. Will this be me someday? Will I be left alone in a facility somewhere, perhaps with no one but the state to track and manage my welfare?

Will no one think to visit me? Without someone to walk through life with, without that person to share a history, memories, and a purpose with, will I be left to live out solitary memories in my own head? What if my memory fails me?

My friend Julianna had to pull me out of this downward spiral of thinking. She first reminded me that I don't know what the future holds. Quite frankly, I don't know if I have a future beyond tomorrow (as if that's supposed to be comforting). Second, she reminded me that I don't know how God will provide. Who knows? There may be a young woman or a young family somewhere in the future who loves old people (including me!) and on whom God lays the desire to adopt me, care for me, and even claim me as their own. It could happen.

I don't believe it now, of course. That's too hard, and Satan is determined to keep me wallowing in fear. This kind of belief is a process, an "I believe; help my unbelief!"[1] kind of belief. But I will choose to believe that someday God will enable me to believe it, and that someday, if it comes to what I described, God will provide. That's a start.

Finally, there's a feeling around being single when you don't want to be. The feeling hits both men and women, though it can manifest itself differently and at different times. That feeling is shame.

You've probably heard it said that guilt is felt as a result of things we've done, but shame is sourced out of our identity—the sense that something is terribly wrong with who we are. I've felt it. I know I shouldn't because I can recite any number of verses on who I am in Christ, and I know all of the corresponding truths in my head. But when my heart is hurting, when I feel like the big scarlet S of singleness is on my chest for all to see, it seems impossible to find and cling to my true self. The lies want to win, and they do everything in their power to do so.

What does shame around singleness look like? You can see it in the following statements:

"In the literally billions of people on earth, I haven't found one who'd like to spend their life with me. It's like I'm in junior high again, waiting to be picked for the team, but no one wants me."

"I'm left out of conversations at church, work, even in my own family, because I can't relate to what they're saying about their spouses, kids, and married life in general."

"I know my parents want grandchildren, but I'm not able to give them their wish. I feel like a colossal failure and that I'm letting my family down."

"People assume I'm gay because I'm not married yet."

"The kids I babysat in high school are now getting married. Me? I can't even get a date."

These are hard things to feel and experience. Very hard. And they lead to questions that ultimately cause us to question our worth and God's goodness. If you ask yourself questions such as *Why am I still single? What's wrong with me? Has God forgotten me? Am I being punished for something in my past? Can I ever be truly fulfilled without marriage and a family?* then you're in good company.

It's one thing to believe God can do something in our lives; it's another thing to believe he actually will. When we have no guarantees, it's easy to let our spirits go to discouragement, doubt, and eventually bitterness.

As I described in my Ferris wheel story in the prologue, it's not that being denied admittance to the Ferris wheel caused me to question God's existence. Not at all. But on that drive home, the feelings that hit me without warning brought up every wound related to my singleness I had ever experienced. As I exited the carnival, I remember looking around me, feeling conspicuous that my singleness was evident to everyone in the park, almost like a neon sign above me read REJECTED.

So what do we do with this grief? Not just when it threatens to engulf us, but when it threatens to steal our day-to-day joy? That's almost more dangerous. That kind of grief eats away at us until we're going through the motions, having checked out of life, relationships, ministry, and more. Better to feel this stuff deeply than stuff it away to do its dangerous work in the dark.

You certainly don't want to beat yourself up. Saying, "If only I'd done this differently or had been more this way or less this way or worked harder at this," will dig yourself a big hole that you'll eventually fall into. Citing all the "if onlys" is counterproductive and crazy-making.

Likewise, shifting blame to others won't help, either. In assessing my history of dating and singleness, I only half-jokingly tell people I blame my twenties on myself, my thirties on men, and my forties on God. Whining about the passivity or cattiness of the opposite sex, chewing out your once-overprotective parents, or ruing the day you read *I Kissed Dating Goodbye* can't change these things now. Get over them.

One hard truth to keep in mind, however, is: you are not guaranteed marriage, no matter how badly you want it or how prepared you think you are for it. God doesn't owe you marriage as a reward for good behavior, be it sexual purity, service on the mission field, or whatever else you may put on your ledger of superspiritual deeds. Nor does God need you as some kind of object lesson to those who have weak faith. He's perfectly capable of showing his glory (and already has) to a world needing evidence of his power and grace. Working a miracle in your love life is not necessarily on the list.

I have friends who dumped loser boyfriends with the assumption that God would notice, applaud, and subsequently (and in record time) reward them with Mr. Right. Their valiant effort to "do good" would be God's cue to step up to the plate and deliver the goods.

Most of these friends are still single. Did God forget to show up? Not at all. God knows what he's up to. He's still in control, but he's on his own timeline and business plan. He has no interest in being the proverbial puppet or vending machine.

So if singleness is hard, and we're not guaranteed marriage, what do we do with all this sadness?

I think the first thing we need to do is grieve.

These are weighty losses. These are issues of the heart. These are fears, dashed dreams, and crushed assumptions, and many of them are laced with lies about ourselves, our circumstances, and even God himself. You don't mess around with this kind of grief.

I love that David tells us in the Psalms to "pour out [our] complaint" to God.[2] Do this first. Going to God, who knows your story and has the power to actually do something about it, makes incredible sense. This is a lot more productive and healing than griping to friends, coworkers, Internet forums, or, heaven forbid, members of the opposite sex whom you'd like to be dating.

Don't worry. God can handle your grief. He can also shoulder your anger, questions, and doubt. He cares about you more than anyone does, and he knows what's best for you. A couple of years ago I did Beth Moore's *Believing God* Bible study. I remember her talking about God in relation to answered prayer and reminding us that when we receive a no to one of our requests, it may be a timing issue, but it may also be the precursor to a bigger yes. Isn't it good to know we serve a God who, at all times, is behind the scenes in our story? We think we know what's best for us, but we're no match for God's eternal wisdom. We're pretty dumb in comparison, really.

So go to God. Let him know where you stand. And don't say, "He already knows, so what's the point?" There's something about getting it out in front of God, whether audibly or on paper, in the quiet of your home or apartment or on a run or bike ride, that gives a measure of comfort and clarity to the situation.

I'm a girl who takes breakups hard. I find this odd, since on the Myers-Briggs Type Indicator I'm an ENTP, and my *T* (thinking versus feeling) is pretty much off the charts. I'd like to think this means I'm always emotionally stable and comfortably low-key, and I usually am, except after a breakup. In that instance, there I am, completely overwrought, taking the breakup personally, overanalyzing it, and doing basically everything I've told you not to do.

After one particularly tough breakup, I knew I'd be in for about a three-month season of grief at least. I also knew I didn't have the capacity for this, didn't want the drama, and knew the relationship and its circumstances didn't merit such an all-out assault on my emotions.

I went to God.

I remember sitting in my living room and bawling. This was not a demure, pretty cry. This was a sobbing, heaving, doubled-over wailing that I didn't know I was capable of. I grieved the end of the relationship. I grieved my attachment to it. I grieved being rejected, and I grieved my aloneness in the wake of it.

I grieved. And grieved. I also asked God—begged, really—to remove my attachment to that relationship, that guy, and all the hopes and dreams I'd built up in it. I poured out my complaint. And I asked for nothing short of deliverance. I spoke it aloud. I asked several times. I was audacious.

And then I got up and put praise music on my stereo. I played it loud and sang along. I went to bed, and the next morning I woke up and, as surely as I sit here, had no feelings one way or the other about that failed relationship. I had no ill will toward my ex, no anger at God, and no despair at my circumstances.

Mind you, this has only happened to me once. I've grieved other relationships in a much messier, more drawn-out fashion. But the fact is, God met me in this one, in part, I think, because I went to him humbly and asked. Try it sometime.

Also, remember: God "is near to the brokenhearted."[3] He doesn't shy away from pain. He doesn't hang out with only the cool kids (praise God!). He's got the hairs of your head numbered.[4] He created you for a reason—and in his image, to boot. He puts the lonely in families.[5] As a child of God, you are engraved on the palms of his hands.[6] Look up these verses, write them down, and memorize them. They are a big deal.

In seasons of doubt, I've also found it helpful to look back and see where in my life God has been faithful. A while back, I wrote a blog post about this and titled it "Thanks for Nothing."[7] In it, I outlined some of the things in my life I have been denied and how (usually months or even years later) I discovered this was ultimately a good thing.

Back in high school I desperately wanted to go to Yale University. I applied, interviewed, and even received welcome literature and information from various campus clubs. But in the end, my application was declined. I went on to attend a Christian university where my faith deepened, I made lifelong friendships, and took opportunities that ultimately led to what I'm doing today.

Thirteen years ago I was diagnosed with rheumatoid arthritis. I figured this incurable and often debilitating disease signaled the end of any sort of meaningful life; it certainly felt as though the door slammed shut on my youth. But what I gained was a compassion for those who suffer and the privilege of trusting God with something beyond my control. And in the midst of it all, God gifted me with miracle drugs (that's at least how I see them) that, for now, have my disease in near remission. To God be the glory.

I turned down a dream job in another state, not knowing that a few months later I'd join an international young-adults ministry, and six years after that I'd be writing this book to the young-adult generation I've come to love.

Romantic relationships tanked and that was hard, but it would've been much worse had they led to marriage. In most cases, they were either bad fits or just flat-out dysfunctional. Praise God for his intervention when I was too dumb or stubborn to admit the truth.

You see—we're often encouraged to be grateful for what we have, but don't forget to be thankful for what you don't have. Thank

God for the "nothing" that is a blessing in disguise. Someday you'll see God's grace in it all.

In the meantime, remember that God is eager to give you good gifts too. "Which one of you, if his son asks him for bread, will give him a stone? Or if he asks for a fish, will give him a serpent? If you then, who are evil, know how to give good gifts to your children, how much more will your Father who is in heaven give good things to those who ask him!" (Matt. 7:9–11).

It's true that many of us are not where we'd hoped to be in terms of marriage. We're feeling cheated and left behind. Our own mistakes and missteps aside, the generations of cultural sin before us have plopped us in a relational landscape that is confused, fickle, and increasingly fragmented.

The fact that anyone still gets married is a miracle. Similar to the terms *God* and *faith*, a common understanding of the word *marriage* can no longer be assumed. We have to cling to what we know from God's Word. We have to choose to uphold marriage even before our own is established. We must fight for purity, fidelity, and the courage to love others boldly.

This must be done even as we wait.

I never wanted to be the poster child for singleness. I certainly never asked for it. But with thousands of single young adults who look to me as an example for weathering—no, *conquering*—an extended season of singleness with grace and dignity, it's where I am.

I called my mom a couple weekends ago, and she asked what I was up to. "Well, I just finished an hour-long radio interview."

"On what topic?"

"Singleness."

"Oh, for Pete's sake! Are you still on that topic? You need to find some lonely man to marry you so you can move on."

Ha-ha. I'd love to, Mom. And I pray to that end. And you know what? As long as I'm alive, there's still hope of it happening. But, thank God, I've learned that I'm okay right where I am too. I'm not less because I'm single. I'm not incomplete. I'm not forgotten, judged, or living under a death sentence. I'm a redeemed and chosen child of God, and he's got good—no, great—things planned for me as I choose to maximize the season I'm in, regardless of what the future holds.

So that's what I'll do.

# CHAPTER 10
# LIVE A LITTLE
# (OKAY, LIVE A LOT)

It was my senior year of college, and our concert choir was on a spring break trip to Florida. We toured up and down the state, performing in various churches and schools that had been scheduled as part of our itinerary.

One of our concerts was at a housing village for retired, and generally quite elderly, missionaries. Think *The Golden Girls* without the fornication, language, and alcohol.

After our concert in the community chapel, we were divvied up among the white-haired, cane-carrying crowd to be housed for the night. Angela, a spunky African American sophomore and fellow alto, and I were assigned to Florence, a simply precious lady who had spent much of her life as a missionary in Venezuela.

Florence was too old to drive, so another one of the seniors had driven her to the concert. This woman was now giving Florence, Angela, and me a ride to Florence's home just a few blocks away.

We chatted easily, and Florence praised the concert, especially the hymn arrangements, because "that's what music is supposed to sound like."

Meanwhile, Angela pulled out a bag of chocolates she had purchased earlier in the day and began passing them around. When the bag was offered to Florence, she demurred, citing her cholesterol, high blood pressure, occasionally high blood sugar, and general need to eat "only what my doctor orders."

Angela wasn't about to take no for an answer. In her characteristic south-Chicago style, she retorted, "Oh, c'mon, Flo—live a little!"

"Flo" dutifully took a chocolate, looking a little sheepish. She then took two more and promptly popped them into her mouth. We all giggled and praised Flo for her recklessness. Angela smiled triumphantly.

Sometimes we have to remember to live a little. Life has a way of bringing us down. Burdens, expectations, responsibilities—they all do their part in shoving us further and further into ruts we promised we'd never fall into back when we were blissfully unencumbered and carefree.

But life has a way of interrupting our dreams and messing with us. Days are consumed with work, school debt, credit card bills, broken or stagnated relationships, and everything else that makes getting up in the morning a tougher chore with each passing day. It's an overwhelming feeling that things may not get better; that maybe this is all there is; that the next ten, twenty, or thirty (please, no!) years will be summed up with one big "meh."

It's time to get unstuck. To remember what's great about where we are now and what we've been given. To really start living, not just existing. To start maximizing the season we're in while still remaining hopeful for what's to come.

An episode of a popular daytime talk show comes to mind. It was years ago, but it stuck with me, because the audience that day was filled primarily with single women. The talk show hostess was asking them what it meant to be single, what their lives looked like in their normal day-to-day routines. I remember one woman saying she had lived in her apartment for years, but had yet to hang any pictures. Why not? Because she was waiting to get married. She didn't want to settle in until then. It's almost as if she feared that embracing her singleness would secure her that status for life. So instead of claiming her space and filling her home with the things she loved, she lived in a state of nomadic uncertainty, waiting for life to happen to her instead of shaping it into what it could be.

Folks, life does not begin at marriage. Singleness is not a waiting room for marriage, where only the lucky ones get called in for an audition.

Don't worry, I'm not going to start in about how Jesus was single, and "don't we all want to be like Jesus?" Give me a break. No one needs to hear that. What I will say, however, is that even if you desire marriage and feel called to marriage, and even if it hasn't happened yet, you can still be a fulfilled, fun, effective, and generally rockin' person while you wait. Because you're not defined by your marital status. You are you. You'll still be you when you get married. Don't tread water while waiting for that person to magically appear. Be the you that you are right now; God made that person, Jesus died for that person, and there's a grand purpose for that person.

Still skeptical? Let me explain.

I think it's easier to be grateful for our own stories when we look at them specifically, not in generalities. A few years ago, I had fourteen friends get married in the span of a year and a half. Fourteen. I attended most of those weddings and was in some of them.

As the invitations started pouring in, my first thought was, *Well, this sucks. Once again, I am the odd girl out as my friends move forward in life.*

But that's when the grace of God stepped in.

Seriously. Looking back, I put that experience in the miracle category. It could've been a horrific season. But God did something in my heart that I can take no credit for. He gave me eyes for my friends' specific stories. By allowing me to separate them from the disappointment and longing in my own story, he showed me how my friends' stories were not my stories, and because their soon-to-be husbands were not my soon-to-be husband, I could be completely and independently happy for each one of them.

It was a weird realization and a unique application of the "rejoice with those who rejoice" mandate of Romans 12:15. God, in giving my friends husbands, was not denying me one. He wasn't holding back from me in order to bless my friends. He doesn't operate with limited resources. It was my friends' time for marriage, plain and simple, not mine.

It's this realization that allowed me to go through a terrible breakup on a Friday night, then show up to a friend's wedding the next morning. There were a few tears, sure, but there was no bitterness, no emotional implosion or gnashing of teeth. I have great memories from that wedding. I would be so bummed if my memories of that day were marred by anger or jealousy. It was a conscious decision to smile that day, but the smiling paid off. The resolute determination to remember that "joy comes with the morning"[1] paid off. Trusting paid off.

A life lived in generalities is defined by stereotypes:

> *Always the bridesmaid, never the bride*
> *Bachelor 'til the rapture*
> *The crazy cat lady*
> *The socially awkward single dude who struggles with conversations beyond Star Wars*
> *The "nice guy" who's always passed over for "bad boys"*
> *The bitter, angry single woman*

In contrast, a life entrusted to the complete, personal, and perfect will of God is content and joyful, living in the now instead of the what if.

So what does that look like for a single person? Because—good news!—being single isn't only about being happy for other people.

I'll start by telling you frankly and specifically what's awesome about my life. And all of this awesomeness is directly correlated to my being single. This is going to sound ridiculously selfish, but it is what it is. This is what makes married people say stuff like, "Why would you ever want to get married?" and "Boy, do I miss the days when I was single. You don't know how easy you have it!"

I don't think these perks are overrated. They're not consolation prizes for missing out on anniversary dinners and the pitter-patter of little feet. I don't think they should be downplayed or apologized for, either. Because being single has its benefits.

First, my time is my own. Besides my general obligations to work, church, and the things I commit to (and, of course, the general understanding that God's really in charge of it all), I decide what I do and when. I plan my weekends based on my wants and needs. I sleep in. I work out at my leisure. I plan outings with friends. I always get my first choice in vacations, because I don't have someone else's schedule or preferences to consider. I go on a cruise because I have the time and can afford it. I've been to Europe, Asia, South America, the Caribbean, and other places. In contrast, I have married friends with young kids who are grateful for the days they can just get out of the house.

Time with my girlfriends? No problem. Dinners, coffee dates, girls' trips, *Downton Abbey* marathons—there's time for them all. I can squeeze in a nail appointment after work, because I don't have to get home to make dinner. I don't even have to eat dinner if I don't want to. I come home from work to a quiet house. I can sit at my computer for an hour watching the latest viral videos and reading my favorite blogs. I go to bed knowing that no one will interrupt my sleep.

Second, I decide where my money goes. Of course, what's God's is God's, but I save and spend based on my own discipline (or lack of it) and choices. I'm the steward of what I have. I create my own budget and (usually) stick to it. If I want to buy those boots, I do. If I'm behind one month on expenses or savings, it's my problem; I have no one to blame.

Third, I have the margin to spend a lot of time in self-reflection. I have the luxury of working on myself in the best possible ways. I write lists, make goals, take assessments, meet with mentors, and go to workshops, classes, and conferences.

I have uninterrupted time with the Lord. I can make a pot of coffee on a Saturday and read my Bible for two hours straight, whereas parents who want to do this have to get up at, oh, four o'clock in the morning; God knew what he was doing in my case. I can pray, journal, or throw on praise music and sing at the top of my lungs with (thankfully) no one to hear me. I can pack a lunch on a whim and drive up to the mountains for a day of hiking and soul-searching.

I'm not saying these things to falsely elevate singleness or justify a life of hedonism or excess. In fact, I'm about to argue why singleness is actually a great season to practice selflessness. I am also not saying that married people can't have nice things, have fun, or be close to God. But the fact remains, singleness has its perks. Big perks that I often take for granted.

So if I have time, resources, and margin as a single but know I'm not to squander everything on selfish pursuits, what do I do? How do I keep a healthy perspective? How do I live for others when I'm tempted (and usually encouraged) to focus only on myself?

It's chilling when I realize how myopic I'm prone to be. My friend Julianna and I went to Walt Disney World last year. You may think that's a weird vacation for two single women. Maybe it is. Don't worry; I'm keenly aware of our need to not become those older single women who ride around on motorized carts wearing Tinker Bell T-shirts and trading Disney pins. I also know many folks probably assumed we were a lesbian couple. Whatever. I love WDW and refused to be deterred.

We were in the Magic Kingdom when my single nearsightedness hit me full force. Sitting at an outdoor food court, it seemed that a higher-than-usual number of pint-sized princesses and pirates were running about. They were squealing, shouting, crying, spilling, pouting, and being—wait for it—kids. I turned to Julianna and blurted, "What is up with all these *kids*?"

Newsflash! Lisa, you're at Disney's Magic Kingdom. There are usually kids there. In fact, you're kind of the outsider. And kids act like kids.

Good reminder.

Married people (and especially those with kids) are reminded daily that life is not about them. They are asked to sacrifice daily. Their attitudes, actions, and wills are tested daily. Their sin is also generally on full display to those they love. But they also reap the rewards of having others who depend on them and love them. They pour into others both by choice and necessity.

I want that too. But as a single person, I have to look for it. Singleness is no excuse to be a lone ranger. By virtue of who I know God created me to be, being reclusive, selfish, unloving, or greedy is out of the question.

God has many ways for me to give. He fully intends me to be stretched and refined too. To think that only happens in marriage is foolish and naïve.

First, I need to seek out relationships. This should begin with my family. Just because I'm an adult doesn't mean I neglect my parents, siblings, and extended family. They're a great place to give and receive the grace of God, and for some of us, they're a tough place to do so.

We need to learn to relate to our family members as adults. This means dealing with and letting go of the baggage we have hauled over from our childhood. It means forgiving. It means caring for our families with the resources we now have. It means not envying or belittling their stories or comparing them to ours.

I have the privilege of helping with caregiving for my mom. Our story has come full circle, with me and my sisters now in the role of meeting her daily needs and helping her finish well. My sisters and I talk on the phone. We go on occasional trips together. We counsel and pray for each other.

Singleness has also taught me the importance of friendship. I sometimes think singles understand friendship better than marrieds; in a way, we have to. If we're going to have deep, meaningful relationships, we have to go after them. We must nurture and care for them and be willing to enter conflict and stay there until it's resolved.

My sister Tina admitted to me a while back that she doesn't have many close friends. She and my brother-in-law are each other's best friend. They've been married forty years *(what?)*, have lived all of that life side by side, and are completely comfortable with each other. For better or worse, they meet most of each other's needs.

I, on the other hand, have only entered "real" relationships in the past decade, and more deliberately in the last few years (after that huge fourteen-friend marriage migration). I've had to work at opening up, loving others unconditionally, and resolving disagreements instead of walking away—all the things you think should come naturally for any normal, functioning adult. But for a single girl, this stuff can be difficult, just as it can be for my sister moving into friendship territory.

The work has paid off. My close friends are now family. They are my tribe. They are my accountability, my shoulder to cry on, my ride to the airport, my pew buddies at church, my chicken soup delivery when I'm sick. They're a ton of fun too.

In reflecting on our hard-won friendships, we've speculated that perhaps singles get into bad dating relationships because they don't have good friendships. Left with a hole to fill, singles panic and start seeking out companionship, love, and acceptance wherever they can find it. Without the accountable care of those who know and love them, they make rash decisions that can lead to heartache down the road.

My friends have my back. They won't let me live life for me only, nor will they leave me to drift into loneliness and despair. I know they know me and care about me, and they know I know and care for them.

Second, your single season is also a great time to serve. There's a reason Paul said that unmarried men and women can, without distraction, be focused on how to "please the Lord."[2] We have time, attention, and energy to give. And there are many great places to invest.

Start by taking a spiritual gifts test if you haven't already. Figure out what you're great at. Then decide what, specifically, you're passionate about. As Bill Hybels says, what's your "holy discontent," that thing that gets you riled up, that makes you want to be part of a solution, change, or renewal?[3]

Find out what's going on in your church or community along these lines. If it doesn't exist, create it. Or you may feel compelled to fill a hole that already exists. Maybe it's a ministry you've never tried or even considered before. Check it out. Churches always have critical needs that must be filled. This may be your time to fill one of them. I've done my share of snack and coffee service; I've filled

Communion cups; I've helped hang drywall. Am I amazing at these things? No. But I can take direction. And when a need is there, I occasionally see it as my turn to step in.

This is also a great time to do missions trips, work projects, and longer-term volunteering. Young adults are often criticized for being lazy, entitled, and unwilling to commit to anything. Here's a chance to prove folks wrong. Set an example à la 1 Timothy 4:12, showing that you're a self-starter who is willing to dig in, get things done, and lead change. You'll turn some heads for sure.

After rehearsing all the great things about singleness, my third point is going to sound weird. But here it is: your single years are a great time to start investing in marriage, both in the marriages around you and your own future marriage.

A while back, I decided I was going to remain in the lives of my now-married friends. It hasn't been easy. Our lives and schedules are very different. Our priorities are different. But I try, because they are still my friends; marriage hasn't changed that, I hope. It's sad when I see blame shifted in these areas. Singles say their married friends dump them for their husbands or wives, leaving them in the dust to feel forgotten and second class. Sometimes this is true; I won't deny it. What's more, being dumped for a spouse is biblical, especially in the first year of marriage.[4] But there are ways to do it well without thumbing your nose at your single friends and making them feel used.

Marrieds sometimes feel dumped by their single friends. Your single buddies no longer invite you over for football or pool, figuring you're stuck on kid duty or obligated to watch *The Notebook* with your wife for the twelfth time. Your single girlfriends go to movies without you, largely because they don't want to accommodate your kids' routine or your babysitting hurdles.

But staying connected to married friends is crucial. So is honoring their marriages. About eight years ago, I decided that I would do everything within my power to honor and protect my friends' marriages. This has a number of different faces. It means babysitting so my friends can get a night out together or finish their Christmas shopping or address an issue that's becoming a problem in their relationship.

It means building up my married friends verbally and publicly, both in front of each other and in front of our mutual friends and acquaintances. Saying what people are doing right in their marriages can go a lot further than dragging out the tired ball-and-chain metaphor in all its forms.

It means praying for my friends' marriages and refusing to gossip about their issues. It's not participating in spousal gripe sessions. It's not joking about marriage or lending credence to those who do. It's vocally reaffirming God's heart for marriage, as well as the people whom he's blessed with it.

Your single season is the best time to start preparing for your own marriage. I can't tell you how many people I know who figured the time to start learning about marriage was when they got engaged. Bad idea. That's like standing at the open door of a plane and asking your skydiving instructor what's on your back and how to use it.

Soak in everything you can right now. Read marriage books. Go to marriage conferences. Interview married couples. Find out what this marriage thing is all about. Singles who see marriage in their future should be passionate about marriage. They should also be students of it. The first few years of marriage are an adjustment—typically an especially tough one. Know what to expect so you can meet it all head-on. Then you can truly enjoy the process.

But don't forget: a built-in bookcase full of marriage books won't get you married. Prepare, prepare, prepare, then act on what you know. If you've truly maximized your season of singleness and have few regrets, you'll be ready to eagerly embrace what's to come.

In the meantime, hang those pictures. Buy new towels. Or buy a home, for that matter. Put down roots and embrace who you are and where you are now. Because the you you are now feeds into the you you're becoming. Maturity, sanctification, fruitfulness, joy—they are the goals for us all; they are not the realm of marrieds only.

# CHAPTER 11
# "GOD IS SOVEREIGN ... SO, WHATEVER"

It was before Sunday school on a crisp autumn Sunday, and members of our class were walking through the door, pouring coffee, milling around, and catching up on one another's weeks.

Then someone brought up the upcoming national election. Immediately the attention in the room was focused on the topic. A debate ensued, causing some folks to take sides. A few began monologues on various policy positions. Comparisons to previous elections were made. There was even (surprise) a character attack or two on both candidates.

Julianna, an informed and somewhat private voter, rolled her eyes at the scene before her. Wanting to change the subject, she spoke loudly, interrupting the individual who currently had the floor. She pronounced, "Look, God is sovereign ... so, whatever."

We all got a good chuckle from that. It's not that she was encouraging people not to vote. Nor was she saying it didn't matter how we vote or why. She was, I think, just trying to assert that in the end, our preferences, patterns—even our substantiated projections—don't mean as much as God's good plan.

This applies to more than politics. It applies to our very lives. And it applies to our current singleness, as well as to our (Lord willing) future marriages.

Everyone is single for a season. Some will be single for a short season. Others, like me, have been single for a longer season. Some will even be single for their entire lives. But the fact is, no season is better than another. God doesn't love married people more.

Nor is singleness a punishment. I've had people ask me if God's withholding marriage from them because they sinned sexually in the past. Divorced friends have wondered if they had their chance at marriage, then when their relationships crumbled, God said, "Sorry, you blew it. Never again."

God's grace is limitless. That means there's grace enough for every one of our stories and the moments that comprise them. God is not hampered by our stops, starts, failures, or limitations. He doesn't wring his hands over our singleness, wondering when we'll get hitched so he can really start blessing us and making us useful for the kingdom.

I really didn't understand this until after I turned forty. I'll be honest; my forties have been no easy transition. I've had to reconcile myself to the fact that I'm no longer a young adult. I'm not the peer of the people I serve. I'm more of a big sister or aunt, though I do my best to be the hip, fun, cool aunt who remains relevant but not too trendy or ridiculous.

But God must've known that forty would be a blow, because he's given me a truckload of grace in the midst of it. You'll remember that I described my thirties in previous chapters as a season of unrest, of making up for lost time and giving too many chances. My forties have been different. I'm more settled, confident, and content with my story. I can see the benefits of singleness as never before. I still see the benefits of marriage, mind you, but marriage is no longer the be-all, end-all it once was.

Just a few days ago my friend Amie and I returned from an East Coast trip to visit our friend Christina, who married the love of her life five years ago. Her husband had three kids when they married, and they now have three more, including a newborn.

Our time with Christina and her family was a blast, but it was no Sandals resort. Amie and I were plopped into the middle of Christina's hectic and demanding life. There was a newborn who slept, cried, ate, and pooped with remarkable frequency. There were two toddlers demanding to be fed, played with, read to, dressed, washed, helped, and generally watched like a hawk to prevent them from killing themselves, us, or the entire neighborhood.

Add to this three teens who were attempting to maximize the final days of summer while getting ready for back-to-school madness, juggling friends, grandparents, and general teen angst, all while helping with the babies and the chores.

And this was with the presence of an incredibly talented and helpful husband who was on paternity leave. I walked away wondering how they do it all. I told Amie on the way home (as I sipped an iced coffee and read the latest issue of *Virtuoso Life*) that for all our griping about singleness, we would call that visit to Christina's our Singleness Affirmation Trip. It was obvious that singleness (at least on that front) is a cakewalk in comparison.

Here's the deal. God knows exactly what he's doing. Does the above story mean Christina made a bad trade when she hung up her single girl status? No way. Does it mean Amie and I would make terrible mothers and should thus avoid marriage (and especially children) at all costs? Absolutely not.

It just means that God meets us right where we are. He gives us grace for our current situations. Sometimes it seems that we don't receive an ounce more than the exact grace we need. Probably a good idea; it keeps us dependent on him.

One of my favorite hymns is "He Giveth More Grace" by Annie Johnson Flint. I especially love this hymn because Annie is a kindred spirit of mine. Like me, she was afflicted with rheumatoid arthritis, though in a time when drugs and treatments were scarce, and an RA diagnosis was at best a complete debilitation, and in many cases a death sentence. Annie knew what she was talking about when she talked about grace for each day. Most days she couldn't get out of bed. The first verse of the hymn says:

> *He giveth more grace when the burdens grow greater,*
> *He sendeth more strength when the labors increase;*
> *To added affliction He addeth His mercy,*
> *To multiplied trials, His multiplied peace.*[1]

Many consider the dating process, the pursuit of marriage, and the interim abiding as a single to be "multiplied trials." For some, they truly are. God never promised this process would be easy.

This brings me to a point about dating that I don't want to forget. Not all dating is a 1950s utopian picture of walking hand in hand to the corner drugstore for a Coke, then stealing a kiss outside your girlfriend's gate before she skips inside, giggling, to pour out everything into her diary.

Dating in today's world is tough. In a culture that is defined by hookups, cohabitation, and delayed marriage, it's easy for singles—even Christian singles—to feel defeated. As we protract our singleness into our late twenties, early thirties, and beyond, we carry with us accumulated baggage and more muddied stories. How do we sort through it all? How do we evaluate potential mates in light of not mere imperfections but downright dysfunctions?

As more and more of my friends go online to find love, I see them wrestle with this very tension. They meet men and women who are divorced, often with kids, sometimes still haggling over custody or visitation rights. Many are wounded. Some are saddled with huge amounts of debt. Others have histories littered with porn addiction, drug addiction, homosexual relationships, multiple sex partners, and more.

If there's redemption there and God's calling my friend into a story that will glorify himself, so be it. But my counsel to them is always this: you don't have to sign up for a mess. God never said we are to get married at all costs. He can sanctify us and magnify himself through our singleness too.

Marriage is tough enough. You should go into it with full assurance that God's in it. You should see his work firsthand. You are not obligated to hang on and hope, pray, and/or nag as your boyfriend or girlfriend struggles to get their stuff together. Let God do his work first and trust him for the outcome. If the relationship is meant to be, both individuals will be ready to approach it healed and whole, with renewed focus and unencumbered by unfinished business.

It's hard, because you may feel that this guy is your last chance at marriage. You may feel you don't deserve marriage at all, so why shouldn't you settle? Who are you to judge? Or that girl is beautiful and vulnerable, and you see her as someone to rescue. Besides, you like her kids, and they seem to like you. Sure, she still sees her ex once in a while, but that will change once you're married.

Don't go there without great caution. God's sovereignty comes into play here too. We have to trust God for good things. Not perfect things, but things and people and relationships that will move us closer to him, not further from him. Sometimes the best medicine for healing life and relationship woes is hard, steady work with the Lord, not another relationship to distract you or act as a panacea for everything that's tough in life. Break it off. Go solo. Do the hard work first; then see what God does with your relationship status, whether with this person or someone else he has in mind for you.

But you have to let go. You have to trust that, regardless of how things look, God holds the end of the story and it is ultimately good. He—not a guy, girl, or relationship—is the impetus for true joy. I have the following quote from Elisabeth Elliot hanging at my desk at work.

*The secret is Christ in me, not me in a different set of circumstances.*[2]

Knowing this gives me full assurance that answers are found within my relationship with Christ, not in whatever "good enough" story I think I should sign up for.

The story of Ruth illustrates this perfectly. Most people parade the book of Ruth in front of singles as some kind of amazing love story. Maybe it is. That said, I've never really understood Ruth and

Boaz as a love story. At all. Here's what I understand: Ruth before meeting Boaz.

If you'll remember, Ruth was a widow. She was a Moabite who had married an Israelite. But he died, and she was left with her aging mother-in-law, Naomi (also a widow), and a widowed sister-in-law. This story has defeat written all over it, because widows were already at the mercy of the community, and Ruth, being from Moab, was on the bottom rung of the cultural hierarchy. Put simply, she was a "nothing" by the standards of her day.

Given this, she did the unthinkable. She chose to return with Naomi to Naomi's people. In the mind of any rational thinker, Ruth just solidified her singleness for life. She may have had a chance at remarriage if she stayed among her own people; going with Naomi was the marriage-prospect kiss of death. Who would want her? She had nothing to offer and nothing desirable about her. She was saddled with not only her own needs and burdens but those of Naomi as well. And Naomi wasn't much help. She was old and depressed.

But Ruth had a bigger story in mind. Because she had a big God in mind. She knew the God of Naomi, because she had made him her God. As a result, she put all of her eggs in his basket. She threw herself on his mercy and trusted him completely.

If you've read the Bible, you know the outcome of the story. Whatever romance it holds (still hard for me to grasp), Ruth meets and marries a man who not only loves God but chooses to love her. He's a man of character and standing, and his proximity and relation to her makes him a good fit for becoming what's known as a kinsman redeemer.

But the main takeaway isn't that God fixed everything and tied it up with a bow (Ruth had suffered a lot of loss in the process, and not all of the details of her and Boaz's journey are given to us), it's that Ruth had the faith to go with God. Not with Naomi, per se, but with God. She saw him as a sure deal. Of course, with this, she entered the lineage of Jesus Christ, and all kinds of things get crazy from there. But that's Ruth's story to tell someday, not mine.

Oh, that I would have the faith of Ruth! Oh, that we all would. Because you know what? We all trust God for something. Some of us even have to trust him with multiple things at once.

Maybe for now you're trusting him with your singleness. You think life would be perfect if you could just get married. Then you'd really start living!

But what happens when you get married and eagerly look forward to starting a family, only to discover you're infertile? What then? Or what if you have some unforeseen and very real issues in your marriage? What if you hit financial hardship? What about that rebellious teen you'll someday have? Or that child born with severe mental or physical disabilities?

We can't even begin to imagine the ways we'll be called upon to trust God in the future. It's in our best interest to throw ourselves upon his mercy and protection right now.

So how am I doing that? I walked through some of the ways in chapter 9. But I also find it immensely helpful to remind myself of some facts.

First of all, God is both all powerful and completely good. This is an indestructible combination. Because of it, God can be trusted. As I said before, if he wants me married, he can get me married. Shoot, if he wants to give me a wacky fairy tale that I couldn't dream up for myself, I'm all in. But I don't want to be in a marriage where God's not front and center. I don't want a marriage where it's all work and counseling and drama and cleaning up messes. I want a marriage that makes me sing and makes God great.

Second, there is no marriage in heaven.[3] I know, I know. This is another thing people tell singles to make us feel better. But it's biblical, folks. Death is a great leveler. For the Christian, we anticipate someday meeting our real Groom, the whole reason marriage on earth has been illustrated as a small, imperfect picture of what's to come. We'll be in perfect relationship with Jesus Christ and with each other. If you're sad about being single, knowing that singleness (and marriage and all the loneliness, strife, fear, and discontentment that come with both) will someday be gone is extremely freeing. Praise the Lord that he thought this ending up!

Finally, God is still at work. It ain't over till it's over, folks. I may get married next year. I may get married at ninety years old. I may never get married at all. Bring it on.

I pray boldly for whatever God wants. I don't know what that is; I just know that if it's what God wants, then I want it too.

I sometimes grieve the fact that I have few people in my life who've walked my whole life story with me. Okay, actually, I have no one. My mom comes the closest, having been in my life for most of its ups and downs. Even my siblings have been in my life only in seasons.

But then there's God. He's walked my whole story with me. He fully intends to walk with me to the end of it and into eternity. He's the only one who will ever be that close to my every memory, hope for the future, and step in getting there. He's it. And who knows what he has next for me?

One of my favorite verses is Psalm 77:19. When I was in Hong Kong last year, I mentioned it to one of the women in the church I was visiting. Before I knew it, she had made me a leather cuff bracelet with the verse inscribed on the inside:

> Your way was through the sea,
>     your path through the great waters;
>     yet your footprints were unseen.

If anyone asks me how I can be content with my story, this is it. God is sovereign, y'all. So, whatever.

# AFTERWORD

## A NOTE TO THE CHURCH, PARENTS, OLD-STERS, AND MARRIED PEEPS IN GENERAL

I hope there are a lot of non-singles reading this book. I also hope you non-singles are reading more than just this chapter. (No? Cheater! Go back to the prologue and start there right now. You need to understand my message to singles in order to understand my message to you.)

When I decided to write this book, one of the first things I knew for sure was that I'd finish it with a word for everyone else—those folks who know and love single adults but don't always quite know what to do with us.

Hey, I understand. No judgment from this corner.

Look, we know what we know. And we gravitate toward what we know. Like attracts like, right? And it's not as if single adults (especially young adult singles) are always the best about reaching across life-stage lines, either. We singletons can easily drift into our cozy cliques and shut out the "foreign" married couples and families around us.

But I've already said enough to the singles. Church leaders, parents and grandparents of single adults, mentor types, and married peeps of all ages, this chapter is for you.

I want to use the following pages to spell out exactly what the single adults in your life need from you, because we need you. And if you don't have a single adult in your life, we need you to fix that. We need you to adopt one or five or twenty of us.

I'm not kidding, nor am I being patronizing. There are very real forces in our world today that threaten to derail the young adult generation at a foundational level. Whether in the area of faith, identity, work, or relationships, the devil is out to confuse and condemn this generation. We've already been saddled with physical, emotional, and ideological baggage from the generations before us, and we've topped off the luggage heap with plenty of suitcases that we packed ourselves. We're weighed down and looking for help.

But in far too many corners, we're not finding it.

There are many reasons for this. Probably too many for me to summarize here. But let me address a few areas I think may get us started. I'll then make the case for you—a married person who has limited time and a tragic underestimation of your own wealth of wisdom—to become the catalyst for change in the lives of the singles around you.

## FIRST, TO THE PARENTS OF YOUNG ADULTS

You may be where my mom was/is, wondering how her daughter, a girl whom she "raised right" and seems to be at least not a total social outcast, is still single. You wonder, *Does she even want to get married? Is she being too picky? Is she too focused on her career?*

Your son may be a young adult, and perhaps he is still trying to find his place in the world. But he's twenty-four and living under your roof, and you're wondering if he'll ever be able to pick a career, stick with it, and eventually support himself and a family of his own—but you don't have enough faith to dream that crazy dream just yet.

You've done everything you can to be involved in your kids' lives. You helped them get into college. You helped them through college. You helped them (emotionally, financially, and more) when they finished college and found they couldn't get a decent-paying job.

For some of you, it may be time to stop helping. The so-called helicopter-parent phenomenon seems somewhat new, but it's really not. It trickled in at the end of generation X's coming of age and put its clutches firmly on the millennial generation. These kids were raised by parents who, in many ways, were fearful to let them fail. They were protected at every turn. They were tutored, coached, praised, and paid into a place of entitlement. It's the number-one thing millennials are accused of by older generations.[1]

In talking to parents of young adults, I've come to realize that many parents have (not intentionally, of course) stunted their kids' growth and independence. For some, it's a too-late realization that they protected their kids from too much growing up, and now their grown children are ill-equipped to venture out into the world and solve their own problems, make their own decisions, and pay their own bills.

I had one mom email me to voice her frustration that after filling out all of her son's college applications and applying for all of his scholarships, he didn't seem appreciative. She had no awareness that doing that amount of work on his behalf was a problem in itself. She went on to say she had even outlined some of his essays for college admission. Is that even legal?

At a seminar I presented, another mom piped up about her daughter causing a small fender bender, and rather than deal with the upset driver of the other car, the daughter called her mom from the crash site and handed the phone over to the other driver, expecting her mom to handle the apologizing and explaining.

By no means am I saying all parents are like this. These are a couple of extreme examples, but they are scarily close to the truth for many young adults and their parents today. I've heard parents admit that one reason they hold so tightly to their adult children, even to the point of keeping them at home and funding their lives (including their entertainment in some cases), is that they fear the empty nest. They fear they won't be able to find themselves apart from their kids, that left alone, rattling around in a big house with no one to care for, comfort, and commandeer, they will have no purpose.

These same parents realize, sometimes too late, that all this coddling has left their grown children in a poor place to marry and start a family of their own. They've enabled a prolonged adolescence, what many sociologists call "adultescence."

When I ask parents about their children's marriage prospects, I'm often met with, "Oh, goodness, they're too young. It's not time yet. I wouldn't want to see them make that kind of commitment at this stage." What stage? Adulthood? Good grief.

Most parents I ask put their children's ideal marrying age in the late twenties, even the early thirties for some.

Why? Because parents haven't grown their kids up. They're parenting twentysomethings who are functionally and emotionally teenagers. Or at the very least, these adults have been allowed to avoid the necessary harsh realities of life—those realities that had our grandparents working three jobs and living in studio apartments to make ends meet. Life didn't stop for that generation. They didn't have the luxury of buying the latest iPhone or going on a ski trip with friends when they had to put food on the table. If they didn't put the food on the table, they went hungry. And so did their kids.

Parents, it's not too late to do what I call "take back your basement." It involves disentangling yourself from the emotional (even codependent) elements of your relationship with your adult child. It means establishing appropriate boundaries in the relationship and setting clearly stated expectations that are to be followed to completion. It basically means treating your child as the adult he or she is.

This may mean charging rent. It may involve cutting off the insurance coverage, phone plan, meal prep, and laundry services you've been doling out. It certainly means stopping the enabling assumptions that have you making your children's decisions, cleaning up their mistakes, and taking on the burden of their responsibilities and commitments.

It may mean asking them to move out altogether.

I know a number of families who coexist with adult children in the home. For young single women, remaining at home until marriage (especially if marriage happens earlier rather than later) may be ideal. There's something to be said for the protection of a family—especially a father—in this circumstance.

But there comes a time when relying on family ties for everything tends to do more harm than good. Young adults need to learn what it looks like to form their own friendships and lean on a cultivated community for accountability and support. They need to actively search for a church home instead of piling into the family minivan on Sundays. They need to feel the pressures of relentless bills, repairs, and to-do lists while enjoying the privilege of setting up a home, offering hospitality, and caring for others. They need to get out from under your spiritual shadow and learn to own, defend, and live out their faith before a hurting world.

If you have an adult child who needs a push from the nest, start the conversation now. But be gentle. Don't throw the entire contents of her bedroom out onto the lawn. Don't demean him or question his character. Show confidence in your child, backed by a hearty dose of love and acceptance.

Make your "it's time to grow up" decisions professional. Draw up a contract, if necessary. Outline your expectations, whether it's for rent, chores, payment of debt, or a move-out date. Be specific, objective, and consistent. Treat your son or daughter as a tenant now, so you can relate to him or her as a family member when it matters.

Do all this, and you'll set yourself up for success in both moving your adult child toward maturity and yourself toward greater sanity. You'll also give your child a healthy nudge toward preparing for the next stage of life, including marriage.

So what if you have a mature, responsible, lives-independently-and-knows-more-about-life-than-you-do young adult, but there's evidence of relationship inertia?

Well, first off, don't pry. Don't constantly ask him, "How's your love life?" or tease her about every ringless man that darkens her social circle. Don't say, "When I was your age, I already had three children," or "Isn't your clock ticking pretty loudly by now?"

If your child wants to get married, he or she is already painfully aware of these things. And if your child doesn't care about marriage, then maybe he's not cut out for it or maybe God has to do some work on her heart to get her there. It's not your job to shame your son or daughter to the altar.

So what can you do?

Start with prayer. Pray fervently and specifically for your adult children. Pray for their hearts, their minds, their purity, their purpose, and their futures. Pray for their future mates. Let your children know you're praying for them. Give them space to share their hearts, and don't badger. Ask good questions. Share from your own mistakes.

Furthermore, encourage them. Your sons and daughters are emerging into a culture of adulthood that is bent on distracting, disillusioning, and demoralizing them. It's set up to make marriages fail. Add to this Satan's desire to basically destroy them (and their future marriages), and you have a bleak picture. Show your kids that marriage is possible and is actually a good thing, especially with Christ at the center.

Take every opportunity to praise progress and maturity in your children. Recognize integrity and doing the hard thing. Discuss finances, relationships, faith, and other real-life issues adult to adult, not adult to child. Practice forgiveness and grace in all things.

Let your children fail. Remember what life was like back when you were figuring things out. Don't expect perfection or perfect agreement. Be willing to cut the apron strings and let go. Cultivate friendships with your adult children built on mutual affection and respect. Then turn them over to the Lord. You now have influence on your children, but not control.

I had a friend who, at her bridal shower, was given a gift from her future mother-in-law. Upon opening it, she pulled out two apron strings. "This is me saying that I'm releasing my son to you," her mother-in-law said. "You and Brian will be one. I will be here to help you, pray for you, and root for you, but I will not be here to interfere. I love you both. My job is done."

That presentation rocked my world. I still get tears when I think about it. What a wise, secure, forward-thinking mom.

Finally, take interest in your children's futures, especially as they date and consider marriage. You may be in a position to suggest potential dates and mates; you may not. Again, don't be pushy. Offer advice when asked. Give your children space and encourage healthy friendships and mentors. Whether because of your history, your or your children's issues, or just your children's temperaments, they may need the influence of other godly adults and couples. Help these relationships happen; don't resort to jealousy or petty anger. Success happens when solid investment happens. Partner with your adult children in investing in their future marriages and families. You'll never regret it, and someday it will most likely pay you back in blessings you never expected.

## OKAY, LET'S MOVE OUT OF THE HOME AND INTO THE CHURCH

Church is a weird place for singles. There, I said it.

I'm becoming increasingly convinced that many churches don't know what to do with single adults. We're misfits, in-betweeners who can't be pinned down, programmed for, or pigeonholed.

It's no secret that the average church today is programmed for families. Look in any bulletin or on any church website, and you'll see mom-centric Bible studies (always in the middle of the work-day), kids choirs, Awana, youth group, and marriage and parenting classes aplenty. Even holidays on the church calendar are planned with families in mind. Whether it's the family Advent workshop, Christmas pageant, or Harvest Festival/Hallelujah Party/Reformation Celebration/Whatever Your Substitute Event for Halloween, church activities love and live for families.

Singles don't have a natural place at these events. We just don't. If we're there, it's because we're serving. I'll bet you've, at some point, seen a single adult lead a high school small group, supervise a bounce house, accompany a choir on the piano, or work in the kitchen. This is good. After all, singles are called to serve too. But it's easy for us to feel used. No single adult wants to hear, "Hmm, there's nothing specific for singles in our church, but would you like to be an Awana leader?"

This lack of connection is why it's hard to find singles at church during the week unless we're serving. For those of us who want community, we have to create it, and this tends to happen outside the structure of the church schedule. Which is a bummer, because for singles who are new to a church, these "underground" events, Bible studies, and small groups aren't publicized, and many single visitors walk away, assuming there's no place for them to fit in. Furthermore, these events are left to operate ad hoc, without the covering and authority of pastors, elders, or mature leaders. This is never ideal.

A few years ago, my longtime singles group at church disbanded. It wasn't the decision of our group; it was the decision of our church leadership. For whatever reason, they chose to no longer support our group as a Sunday school class or church community. They removed us from the teaching schedule and reassigned the elders who had been our overseers, men (and their wives) whom we'd grown to love and consider part of our lives.

I know the decision wasn't made flippantly, and I'm not even sure I totally disagree with it. Our group had begun to evidence some unhealthiness, some imbalance in leadership and investment among its members. Fair enough. But the way the whole thing went down was sudden, final, and, according to most, lacking in compassion and care. Our group members were told to find other Sunday school classes and small groups, to work at fitting in elsewhere—namely, the groups populated primarily by marrieds with children in entirely different stages of life than us.

I'm not here to stump for singles groups. I actually have a love/hate relationship with them. As I mentioned above, they can breed unhealthiness and even become churches unto themselves as the members fence themselves into a singles ghetto of sorts that rarely steps into the larger life of the church. This is not okay.

Ideally, I believe in an integrated church, one where all generations and life stages speak into the experiences of one another. Where the elderly, marrieds, singles, teens, and children worship, study, and serve side by side. Where we pray for one another, break bread together, bear each other's burdens, and share our unique wisdom (or ignorance) and life lessons at a common table.

That said, gatherings of singles within the church certainly have their place too. When I first moved to Colorado Springs, I didn't know a soul. I was desperate to start over (well really, to start, period). I packed my tiny red Mazda with everything I owned and planted myself in the shadow of Pikes Peak. What I didn't bring with me were friends. I was a thousand miles away from my family and in desperate need of community. But community doesn't just happen; it takes time. In the interim are many nights of takeout, Netflix, and social media stalking. It gets old fast. Sometimes I would throw on a coat and drive to the mall just to wander among people (but I bought too many Lancôme cosmetic products this way and had to stop). I cleaned my shower every weekend because I didn't have other plans. I went to movies alone.

That is, until Amie invited me to her Bible study. She'd heard I was new in town and wondered if I may want to meet some women my age. Boy, did I. I started attending and, fifteen years later, those women are still my friends.

As I said in a previous chapter, singles need a tribe to belong to. Because of school or job opportunities, many of us have uprooted and started over in new towns and cities, away from our families and other support systems. We're alone in the world in more ways than one. On Sundays after church, when the families pile into their minivans to head home for lunch and naps, we walk to our cars alone.

Families go to church together. They go to Costco together. They go to soccer practice, McDonald's, and movies together. Even when they expand beyond their family circle, it's usually with other families in the same life stage so that the kids can play together and the parents can talk about parent-type stuff, like Costco, soccer practice, and the age-appropriateness of the latest Happy Meal toy.

In the same way, my single friends are my peeps. They're my tribe. They're my main social circle and support. Giving space for singles to form deep friendships is a win for any church. Jeff Myers, in his book *Grow Together*, says that the value of friendship is so important to millennials, in particular, that if a church doesn't support and provide structure for relationship-building among this generation, it'll be hard-pressed to keep those young adults in its pews.[2]

But singles hanging out with other singles is only part of the equation. Remember what I said about an integrated church that accurately reflects the diversity of the body of Christ? That's important too.

How do we get there, especially as it relates to the single adults in our churches? A good start is understanding singles in general.

A few years back, a couple of single girlfriends and I saw a program advertised in our bulletin at church. Designed to reflect the Titus 2 model of older women mentoring younger women, it assigned a few younger mentees with a (usually) older, spiritually mature woman in the church for the purpose of discipleship and life-on-life impact.

Eager to connect with and learn from someone, my friends and I signed up and were assigned to Kathy, a fiftyish married woman in our church.

Our first meeting was in her home, and as we sat around her dining table, she launched into a short speech. "You should know up front that you women terrify me," she began.

Um.

My friends and I looked at each other, wondering if Kathy was joking. She wasn't.

"The thing is, my heart is for moms with young children. I raised two sons and that's what I know. I was hoping to be assigned a few young, married moms that I could mentor." Almost as an apology, she tacked on, "But I'm sure we'll have fun too."

She didn't look convinced. We found out in talking with her that she felt pretty uncomfortable with the idea of mentoring single girls. She married young and her assumptions about us were that we lived exciting, fast-paced lives with amazing careers and varied experiences. She wondered what she had to offer us. After all, she had "only" been a stay-at-home mom. She knew diapers, carpools, and football practice. She feared that was all she knew.

But we had to tell her that *she* was where we wanted to be. We three eager singletons desired marriage and family. We wanted to learn her story so someday we might have a similar one. It was almost as if she couldn't believe us. It took a lot of convincing on our part to get her to accept her story as one that was valuable to us. It also was a big job to show her that *single* isn't synonymous with *alien*.

I see similar reactions to Kathy's throughout the church.

For the most part, the church doesn't know what to do with singles, largely because the visible majority of church members have moved beyond singleness and lost touch with the needs, attitudes, and aspirations of single adults.

Some, like Kathy, put singles in the "way too cool for me" category. Others do the opposite. They put us at the proverbial kids table.

You know that table. At Thanksgiving and other large gatherings, it's the second-class accommodations reserved for the youngest family members. Usually a card table or piece of plywood balanced on two sawhorses and covered with the extra Star Wars tablecloth from Billy's birthday party last year, the kids table is that space to which those who don't need to be impressed are banished.

For kids, this is a fun place to be. They can talk with their mouths full, squirm, and throw rolls at each other. For adult singles who are placed there because, well, they're just one person and the grown-up table has an even number of seats, the implications are less than ideal.

The kids table mentality transfers into the church too. My sister Sara, bless her heart, showed this all too clearly. When told that my single friends and I had volunteered to sign up for a work project at church, she exclaimed, "That's so great that you can do things with your youth group!"

Yeah, great. Except that we were all in our thirties, not in high school.

A simple mistake but an important one. Just because we're single doesn't mean we're immature or haven't arrived. Most single adults are contributing, functioning members of society and the church and deserve to be treated that way. We're not leftovers from the student ministry, nor are we (unless proven otherwise) slow or in need of special accommodations.

I'm reminded of a time I visited a church and inquired at the visitors desk about a Sunday school class for my age and stage. "Of course," the sweet woman at the desk replied. "We have a class for singles and those with special needs and developmental disabilities. Dave here [gesturing] can bring you there."

Want to love singles in your church? Invite us to the grown-up table. Give us the breakable glasses, not plastic, and let us join in the adult conversation. You may actually learn something from us. And we will be more than willing to jump in and contribute.

Pastors and church leaders, ferret out your single adults and get to know us. Invite us into the life and leadership of the church. Put us on committees. Challenge us to give financially. Ask us to lead a project. Don't let us occupy the sidelines. Make us assimilate.

Also, use us in sermon examples. Not all useful examples center around marriage or parenting. Mention us in congregational prayer. Reference our struggles. Act as if we exist, because we do.

When it comes to cross-generational relationships within the church, I often remind both singles and marrieds that marriage begins with two single people. Hey, we're important! And whether singles eventually move toward marriage or stay single for life, we're still family. What's more, we need families. If we don't have our own, we may need to adopt yours. Will you let us?

There are a few reasons why singles need the larger life of the church. It's a two-way street, but I'll focus on our needs and someday a married person can write the book that tells singles how we can help y'all. Fair enough?

First, singles can't learn everything from singles. Duh. Nor can young adults learn everything from other young adults. To think that we're an island unto ourselves and can operate healthily under that construct is both arrogant and misguided.

For one thing, we just don't know enough. We need older, seasoned believers to get up in our business and tell us what's what. We need to know where you've walked and what you've learned from the journey. We need a glimpse into your life to see that it's not perfect, either. It, like ours, is rife with missteps, disappointments, redirects, and cycles of sin and repentance. We need those folks who are just a few steps ahead of us to turn around and shine the flashlight on the trail beneath our feet.

But here's the problem: fewer and fewer folks are willing to do this. I'm constantly railing on my Boundless audience to go out and get a mentor. I think I've finally driven it far enough into their skulls. The problem is, they're coming back to me, saying, "Lisa, we're trying, but no one's willing to take us on."

Seriously? Empty nesters, where are you? Retirees, surely you have some time. Even you crazy-busy young families have room to invite someone in. We're all called to pour into the lives of others. And you don't have to be Tim Keller or Beth Moore to do it. You don't have to be a biblical scholar or hostess extraordinaire. Everyone has time to sit with someone for a meal or cup of coffee. Moms, let that single woman pop over and watch you throw in a load of laundry. Hey, she may even do it for you and then help watch your kids while you get stuff done. Men, grab that single guy when you go shooting or fishing or to The Home Depot. Everyone has something to give. Just start a conversation. Start small. Can't meet every week? Meet once a month. Don't get legalistic about it, just do what you can. The point is to do it.

When you're planning your week or month, think about how you can enfold a single adult into it. Invite us for dinner after church. Make extra room at your Thanksgiving, Easter, or Christmas table for those who can't get home to family. Send us flowers and a note (maybe just the girls—this could creep guys out) on Valentine's Day, letting us know we're not forgotten.

Show us the loving care of true community. Again, this is particularly important for single women. Men, you have a huge role here. Volunteer to fix things around their houses. Offer your expertise or advice. Stand in as a father figure for women who don't have a dad around. Bonus points if you don't wait to be asked, because single women are afraid to ask. We already struggle with feeling unwanted. We don't want to be a burden. Help us change that. Call the single women in your church and say, "What can I help you with?" Maybe they don't even know. Offer to take a look around their place for things that need to be fixed.

I've had men in my church help me buy a car, fix appliances, walk me to my car after evening activities at church, research and purchase computers, and more. It has meant so much to me that, once again, I'm tearing up as I type.

For single guys, they may need a few extra dinner invitations or even a standing one. They need the friendship of older, married men and the influence of those men's wives. Single men value career and financial advice. Ask them what they need, or maybe tell them. I had one single guy friend who said a man from church called him up and said, "I'd like to get to know you. I'm available for breakfast on Tuesdays or Fridays. Pick one." Startled, my friend accepted. Years later, they still meet on Friday mornings.

Finally, we need the church to help move single adults toward marriage and family. In other words, we need you to get into the business of godly matchmaking.

The church has really dropped the ball on this one. But it's not entirely its fault.

Singles and the church at large are in a catch-22 here. On one hand, the church doesn't talk to singles much about marriage. In an effort not to make us feel bad (a good thing), the church has chosen to remain silent with singles on relationships and marriage (not a good thing). The problem is, most singles want to be married. But the other problem is, we're embarrassed to admit it. Why? Because when we do, we get shamed and preached at.

You can see why this all gets crazy.

Back when I decided I needed to publicly admit my desire for marriage, I gingerly and quietly plopped the idea into the laps of those with whom I thought it would be safe: the married women at church.

Big mistake.

Immediately I was assaulted with some of the most ridiculous and unbiblical things I've heard in church to this day. Here are some examples.

"The last thing you want to think about right now is marriage."

"When you stop thinking about marriage, that's when God will bring someone to you."

"Maybe you're not spiritually mature enough to marry."

"Go on another missions trip. That'll get your mind off marriage."

"I wish I were still single. Wanna trade?"

These were all said by Christian women, many of them long-time believers, Bible study leaders, elders' wives, and/or women in other places of authority.

I felt so foolish. If it wasn't good to desire marriage, then I figured I'd better just keep my mouth shut. I certainly didn't want my fledgling hope to be dismissed so easily. I'd either have to nurture it in secret or try to squelch it altogether.

Many singles have done just this. We've shut down. We've tried to reprogram ourselves. We hold others at arm's length on this subject because we don't want to get hurt.

Because we're staying silent, even the well-meaning married folks are staying silent too. Not wanting to offend, you stay away from subjects like dating and the path to marriage. "I'm not going to interfere in someone's love life," you say.

But that's exactly what we need you to do.

It's what folks did a few generations ago. Back in the day, it was families and church communities that brought couples together. They put pressure on the men to pursue. They encouraged the women to respond. They talked up marriage and communicated the assumption that it was good and for most people. They got involved; they got their hands dirty. Now we've left singles to their own devices. Singles are online or going to speed-dating sessions or random meet-ups.

It's time to bring dating and marriage prep back into the church. "Well, tell the singles that," you say. Oh, I did. And I will.

"I don't want church to be a meat market," the singles say. This is so dumb. It's only a meat market if you let it be. What it is, is a biblical community called to glorify God and enjoy him forever. The path to marriage can be part of that. And married couples and families within the church need to be part of that.

So what does this look like? It starts with befriending singles in your church. It also starts with a heart to see godly matches made. We don't need busybodies who want the Matchmaker of the Year award. We do need tender hearts and wise spirits to help us shape and guide the process.

When approaching singles on the subject, going after men and women may look different. Opening a space for dialogue on dating and marriage is key. Talk it up. Share your vision. Recount your story. Maybe do a small group for singles on the subject.

Then get specific. For women (especially those who've been burned), asking, "Why in the world are you still single?" is not helpful. One of the best ways to open the subject is simply saying, "How can I pray for you?" Let your single friend guide the conversation and share as she's willing. Ask her generally what she thinks about dating and marriage. Ask her what she's seeing in her generation and among her friends.

When guys talk to guys, sometimes a more direct approach is warranted. According to my guy friends, the only generally comfortable subjects for men are sports, hobbies, money, politics (to a point), and the weather. Good luck weaving marriage into those conversations. You may need to just be abrupt and put it out there.

Again, men respond well to challenge but primarily from other men. Suggestions from older married women can help, but a direct question from another man will get heard. Pressure, shaming, and nagging from single women—forget it.

So that said, men, don't be afraid to challenge your single friends on their singleness. If they want to be married, what are they doing about it? Who's in their spheres? Are they praying about potential matches? Are they getting in a position to marry if they're not already?

What are you doing to help them? Are you partnering with them in prayer? Are you suggesting women of character you know? Are you nudging them toward asking women out? Are you instilling confidence in them that it can be done? You have the potential for huge influence here; use it. I truly believe that godly and proactive men can turn our churches around in this and other areas. It's time to get bold and get busy.

Let's bring safety back to the church on this subject. Let's encircle our single adults and show them they're included, loved, and valued. Let's root for them. Let's challenge them. Let's have high expectations of them.

Single young adults are the future of the church. They're also our future marriages and families. They deserve not to be forgotten.

# NOTES

## CHAPTER 1: WHERE DID I GO WRONG?

1. Mark Regnerus and Jeremy Uecker, *Premarital Sex in America: How Young Americans Meet, Mate, and Think about Marrying* (New York: Oxford University, 2011), 169.

## CHAPTER 2: WHAT'S THE BIG DEAL ABOUT MARRIAGE?

1. Candice Watters, *Get Married: What Women Can Do to Help It Happen*, (Chicago: Moody, 2008), 67.
2. Andrew J. Cherlin, "In the Season of Marriage, a Question. Why Bother?" *New York Times*, April 27, 2013, Sunday Review, SR7.
3. Gary L. Thomas, *Sacred Marriage: What If God Designed Marriage to Make Us Holy More Than to Make Us Happy?* (Grand Rapids, MI: Zondervan, 2002), 13.

4. Linda J. Waite and Maggie Gallagher, *The Case for Marriage: Why Married People Are Happier, Healthier, and Better Off Financially,* (New York: Broadway Books, 2001), 64.

5. Genesis 2:24; Hebrews 13:4; 1 Thessalonians 4:3–5; 1 Corinthians 7:2; Ephesians 5:3. For a more thorough exploration of this topic, I recommend *Sex and the Supremacy of Christ* by John Piper and Justin Taylor; *The Meaning of Marriage: Facing the Complexities of Commitment with the Wisdom of God* by Timothy and Kathy Keller; *The Mingling of Souls: God's Design for Love, Marriage, Sex and Redemption* by Matt Chandler; and *The Ring Makes All the Difference: The Hidden Consequences of Cohabitation and the Strong Benefits of Marriage* by Glenn T. Stanton.

6. Glenn T. Stanton, *The Ring Makes All the Difference: The Hidden Consequences of Cohabitation and the Strong Benefits of Marriage* (Chicago: Moody, 2011), 11–12.

7. More than four million US single-mother households live below the poverty level. Hope Yen, "4.1 Million Single-Mother Families Are Living in Poverty: Census," *Huffington Post,* September 19, 2013, www.huffingtonpost.com/2013/09/19/single-mother-poverty_n_3953047.html.

8. Edward Westermarck, *The History of Human Marriage* (New York: Allerton, 1922), chapter 1; and Kathleen Gough, "The Origin of the Family," *Journal of Marriage and Family,* 33, (November 1971): 760–61.

9. D'Vera Cohn et al., "Barely Half of U.S. Adults Are Married—A Record Low," Pew Research Center, December 14, 2011, www.pewsocialtrends.org/2011/12/14/barely-half-of-u-s-adults-are-married-a-record-low/.

# CHAPTER 3: DITCH THE HOLLYWOOD SCRIPT

1. Scott Croft, "Brother, You're Like a Six," Boundless.org, June 1, 2012, www.boundless.org/relationships/2012/brother-youre-like-a-six.

# CHAPTER 4: FIVE REASONS YOUR LOVE LIFE IS A DISASTER (OR DOESN'T EXIST)

1. Marist Poll, "'It's Destiny!' Most Americans Believe in Soul Mates," Pebbles and Pundits (blog), Marist Institute for Public Opinion, February 10, 2011, www.maristpoll.marist.edu/tag/soul-mates.
2. Stanton, *The Ring Makes All the Difference*, 107–25.

# CHAPTER 5: ARE YOU MARRIAGEABLE?

1. Candice Watters, *Get Married: What Women Can Do to Help It Happen*, (Chicago: Moody, 2008), 121.
2. Candice Watters, "Should I Give Up My Missionary Work to Try to Find a Husband?" Boundless.org, August 17, 2009, www.boundless.org /advice/2009/should-i-give-up-my-missionary-work-to-try-to-find -a-husband.
3. Hebrews 10:24–25; Acts 2:42-47; 6:1–4.
4. Romans 12:18.

## CHAPTER 6: PREVENT DATING DEATH

1. Scott Croft, "What Do I Do If a Guy I'm Not Interested in Asks Me Out?" Boundless.org, November 14, 2012, www.boundless.org/advice /2012/what-do-i-do-if-a-guy-im-not-interested-in-asks-me-out.
2. Carolyn McCulley, "Crush Catalyst," Boundless.org, July 28, 2009, www.boundless.org/relationships/2009/crush-catalyst.
3. McCulley, "Crush Catalyst."

## CHAPTER 7: "SOOOO, HOW DO I ACTUALLY START DATING?"

1. Ephesians 5:22–24; 1 Corinthians 11:3.

## CHAPTER 9: IT'S OKAY TO GRIEVE

1. Mark 9:24.
2. Psalm 142:2.
3. Psalm 34:18.
4. Matthew 10:30; Luke 12:7.
5. Psalm 68:6.
6. Isaiah 49:16.
7. Lisa Anderson, "Thanks for Nothing," Boundless.org, November 25, 2010, www.boundless.org/blog/thanks-for-nothing.

## CHAPTER 10: LIVE A LITTLE (OKAY, LIVE A LOT)

1. Psalm 30:5.

2. 1 Corinthians 7:32–34.

3. Bill Hybels, *Holy Discontent: Fueling the Fire that Ignites Personal Vision* (Grand Rapids, MI: Zondervan, 2007), 25.

4. Deuteronomy 24:5.

## CHAPTER 11: "GOD IS SOVEREIGN . . . SO, WHATEVER"

1. Annie Johnson Flint, "He Giveth More Grace," public domain.

2. Elisabeth Elliot, *Keep a Quiet Heart* (Ann Arbor, MI: Vine, 1995), 20.

3. Matthew 22:30.

## AFTERWORD: A NOTE TO THE CHURCH, PARENTS, OLDSTERS, AND MARRIED PEEPS IN GENERAL

1. Nick Gillespie, "Millennials Are Selfish and Entitled, and Helicopter Parents Are to Blame," *Time*, August 21, 2014, time.com /3154186/millennials-selfish-entitled-helicopter-parenting.

2. Jeff Myers, *Grow Together: The Forgotten Story of How Uniting the Generations Unleashes Epic Spiritual Potential* (Manitou Springs, CO: Summit Ministries, 2014), 56.

# GROUP DISCUSSION QUESIONS

## CHAPTER 1: WHERE DID I GO WRONG?

1. How do you feel about where you are in life right now? Are you where you thought you'd be in your education or career? What about your relationships? What decisions (or nondecisions) have led you to the place you are today? Do you feel you need to do anything differently moving forward?

2. What is your current view on dating? What about marriage? How did you come to these conclusions?

3. What are you hoping to get out of this book?

## CHAPTER 2: WHAT'S THE BIG DEAL ABOUT MARRIAGE?

1. Is marriage a priority in your life right now? If so, how? If not, why not?

2. After reading this chapter, what do you see as God's purpose for marriage, and why is it important?

3. What does it mean for you to honor marriage (Hebrews 13:4) even as a single person?

4. How do you feel about the idea "marriage is for most people"? Is it freeing or frustrating?

5. Describe your views on sex. How have your views been shaped, and how do they match up to the claims of the Bible? Do you struggle with feelings of shame about current or past sexual thoughts or behavior? If a virgin, do you have feelings of pride or entitlement?

## CHAPTER 3: DITCH THE HOLLYWOOD SCRIPT

1. If you were to make your ideal love story into a movie script, how would the story play out? Are any of your expectations based on our culture's view of love and romance? If so, how?

2. What qualities are on your "wish list" for a mate? Are these qualities realistic? Are they biblical? How might your list need to be changed after reading this chapter?

3. Describe the fears or regrets that keep you from taking risks in life and relationships. What do you need to do to prioritize a healthy relationship over a pretty face, a project, or an impossible ideal?

## CHAPTER 4: FIVE REASONS YOUR LOVE LIFE IS A DISASTER (OR DOESN'T EXIST)

1. Do you believe in the concept of the One? Why or why not? How do your views on the idea of a "soul mate" affect the way you date or anticipate potential relationships?

2. Which, if any, of the *five reasons* do you see in your own life? Describe how you got to this spot. How does it make you feel?

3. What steps can you take to get unstuck from any unhealthy relationship patterns?

## CHAPTER 5: ARE YOU MARRIAGEABLE?

1. Describe being "in a position to marry." What does this mean for you, specifically?

2. Describe the marriage examples you had growing up. Have they positively or negatively affected your confidence in moving toward marriage yourself? Explain.

3. Of the six qualities mentioned as necessary to maturity, which need some attention in your life right now? What next steps can you take to move forward in these areas?

# CHAPTER 6: PREVENT DATING DEATH

1. Visualize your role in the dating process. What does it look like? Does anything about your current mindset or attitude need to change?

2. Respond to this quote from Carolyn McCulley: "Men trust God by risking rejection; women trust God by waiting." How can this play out practically in your own dating experience?

3. How can men and women appropriately apply an active pursuit of dating to their own roles and responsibilities in the process?

4. Who in your life can you trust to be on your "dating team"? What will it take to assemble this team and put it into action?

# CHAPTER 7: "SOOOO, HOW DO I ACTUALLY START DATING?"

1. How do you define the word *dating*? Do you think there's a commonly understood definition that exists? Why or why not?

2. What are your biggest frustrations with dating? What confuses you?

3. Describe your experience (or nonexperience) with dating up until now. What, if anything, has tripped you up along the way? Do any patterns emerge as you think about this?

4. In what ways could you stand to grow when it comes to relating to the opposite sex? How will you go about pursuing that growth?

5. What is your current commitment to sexual purity? How can you better safeguard your mind and heart, both now and if/when you start dating?

# CHAPTER 8: GET YOUR NUMBERS UP

1. Do you date more or less than you'd like? What factors play into this?

2. Do you ever feel the pressure of too many options? Explain. How do you respond to this pressure?

3. Think about your daily routine—where you work, play, go to church, etc. Are your current habits and activities conducive to meeting new people, especially those of the opposite sex? Why or why not?

4. Which of the ideas suggested in this chapter might you try in order to mix things up and get out of a rut? Write down a couple of possibilities, along with a corresponding plan for getting started.

5. What's your opinion of online dating? What has influenced this opinion?

6. If you've tried online dating, what steps can you take to make the process more intentional and effective?

# CHAPTER 9: IT'S OKAY TO GRIEVE

1. What losses have you experienced in conjunction with being single? Have you ever spent time processing and grieving these losses?

2. What, for you, is the hardest part of being single? In what ways do you feel most misunderstood as a single person?

3. In what ways do you either beat yourself up or blame others for your singleness?

4. Take a moment to reflect on your current situation with all its fears and hurts. Either in prayer or on paper, take the psalmist's advice and "pour out your complaint" to God. Afterward, reflect on the emotions or thoughts that surfaced. Did anything surprise you?

# CHAPTER 10: LIVE A LITTLE (OKAY, LIVE A LOT)

1. Start a list of blessings you see in your life right now. How many of them are directly tied to the stage of life you're in and the unique opportunities that are yours?

2. What does it mean, practically, for you to "rejoice with those who rejoice"—especially those who may be experiencing things in life (like marriage) that you are not?

3. How can you train yourself away from selfishness as a single person? What would it look like for you to live more sacrificially right now?

4. How important are friendships in your life? Do you have at least one or two people who know and love you well, who are willing to confront you and hold you accountable? How can you grow toward the goal of deeper, more authentic friendships?

5. What does it look like to prepare for marriage even while you're single? What advice can you seek out from others? What books might you read?

# CHAPTER 11: "GOD IS SOVEREIGN ... SO, WHATEVER"

1. Do you see your singleness as a short or long season? Are you content with this? If not, why not?

2. Picture yourself in God's bigger story—a story that involves the past, present, and future, all the way into eternity. How do you fit into that story right now? What can you take from an understanding of God's purpose for everything that involves you?

3. What does it mean to give your deepest needs to a God who is both sovereign and good?

4. What is your biggest takeaway from *The Dating Manifesto*? What can you do, beginning right now, to implement positive changes in your attitude and actions regarding dating and the path to marriage?

# AFTERWORD: A NOTE TO THE CHURCH, PARENTS, OLDSTERS, AND MARRIED PEEPS IN GENERAL

1. What assumptions do/did you hold about singles and singleness?

2. In thinking of the singles you know, what challenges do you face in getting to know them and invest in them?

3. Parents, what does your relationship look like with your adult child? What needs to change to grow and mature this relationship?

4. How can the church better serve and equip single adults? How can you, specifically, be part of this process?

5. Write down the names of a few singles in your church. Think of ways you can invite them into your life as their friend or mentor. Write down even the smallest steps to get you started.

6. How can you advocate for marriage among the young adults in your church? What does it look like for you to "help make good matches" among the marriage-minded singles in your sphere? Is the way you talk about marriage (specifically *your* marriage) helping or hindering this?

FOR MORE #HILARIOUS RESOURCES, VISIT:

LISACANDERSON.COM

*(YOU WON'T REGRET IT!)*